# Blue
## HORIZONS

*By the same author*

Bolts From The Blue
Blue Heaven

# Blue HORIZONS

**Rabbi Lionel Blue**

Hodder & Stoughton

LONDON SYDNEY AUCKLAND TORONTO

# Illustrations by Albert Rusling

British Library Cataloguing in Publication Data

Blue, Lionel
    Blue Horizons.
    I. Title
    828'.91402

    ISBN 0-340-50202-9

First published in Great Britain 1989

Published by Hodder and Stoughton,
a division of Hodder and Stoughton Ltd,
Mill Road, Dunton Green, Sevenoaks, Kent TN13 2YA
Editorial Office: 47 Bedford Square, London WC1B 3DP

Photoset by Rowland Phototypesetting Ltd,
Bury St Edmunds, Suffolk

Printed in Great Britain by T.J. Press (Padstow) Ltd,
Padstow, Cornwall

To Linda who packages me, and Ian who lets me talk and talk and talk about it.

To Eva, Kim, Jim, Gordian, Elizabeth, Daphne, Jaap and Theo who holidayed with me and still stayed friends.

To those who holidayed with me and didn't – sorry!

To Hetty who types for me, to Lily who unpacks and folds for me, and Inge who sorts out my confusion of correspondence.

Thank you!

# Contents

7

# *Acknowledgments*

The author and publishers would like to thank Sebastian Temple and the Franciscan Communications Centre for permission to reproduce 'All That I Am' on page 142.

# *Introduction*

My ancestors, spiritually speaking, were devout but static (like battery hens) and died with the same beliefs and attitudes they were born into. My grandparents were immigrants, who had to travel too much in their life, and hoped religion would make the world stand still – at least on the Sabbath.

I, and many of my generation, were more unsettled and free-range. The drawbridge was down, and into our religious ghetto flowed all the faiths and doubts of the outside world, through the wireless, the newspapers, the picture palaces and later, much later, our TV sets. Religion was no longer our fortress but a road, and we were pilgrims on it, singing modern hymns, which suited our situation, such as 'It's A Long Road To Freedom', or 'One More Step Along The World I Go'. To these we had to add the tragic songs of our time, sung by family and friends, whose life's journeys led them through labour and concentration camps – 'Az du gehst den letzten Weg' or 'I Journey Home'.

My journey, thank God, has never passed through these terrible valleys of death. Unlike distant cousins, I

11

have wandered to pleasant places, to seaside piers in Britain, to paella and plonk celebrations on Spanish beaches, and to canteens in Broadcasting House, queueing for my BBC coffee. I've enjoyed the ambulance and trolley rides in hospitals, because I was trundled around with care and kindness.

But hitching beside hedgerows, or watching the flight boards in departure lounges, I've realised that my journey too is divine, though it is not tragic. We come from God, and, please God, we travel towards Him. He (or She) is the purpose and meaning of our journey. In other words, I've rediscovered the road-lore that Bunyan's pilgrim knew three hundred years ago, and the Psalmist almost three thousand.

Many of these travel guides and tips have helped radio listeners keep their calm as they are snarled up in the morning traffic jams, or waiting for transport that never comes, and I hope they do the same for you on some crowded Costa or British beach.

But because I am Jewish, my journey is lightened by more jokes than Bunyan and they will sweeten the serious bits in this log of a modern, accident-prone traveller through life.

# *Arrivals and Departures*

The rabbis said two thousand years ago 'This world is a corridor or vestibule. Prepare yourself in it before you enter the inner room!'

That is how the world seems to me too – a waiting room, an in-between sort of place, which you leave quite suddenly with your newspaper unread, and bits of baggage left behind.

Arrivals and departures, airports, bus stops, setting sail and travellers' cafs are therefore important for me spiritually. They are the time and place when two worlds meet, not just home and abroad, but this world and the next.

That is why I sit in waiting rooms, waiting not only for a plane or train, but also for enlightenment. I study the faces of my fellow travellers and the changing signboard and suddenly it comes.

# Guardian angel at Gatwick

In Gatwick airport, beyond the departure desk, lies Gatwick Village with its hamburger hostelry and chapelette with inter faith furnishings.

I sidled in because my flight was late, but sat up during the sermon. 'Did we know,' the preacher said, 'that each plane carried twice the number of passengers that had checked in?' No I didn't and didn't want to!

He continued. 'Invisible presences without boarding passes come with us. They are our guardian angels.'

I relaxed and laughed. My guardian angel! I hadn't thought of him since the Blitz – when he made me sleep more securely.

Amused, I invoked his presence. He could come with me to Rome where he could meet lots of other angels, adult ones taking off from towers, or blowing trumpets on marble tombs, and fat baby ones adjusting their diapers on frescoes.

Now I don't know who angels are, what they are, or even whether they are, but their presence does make a difference.

While I was with a group down in the catacombs, we saw something small and alive twittering beside a tomb. Someone said soothingly, 'It's only a bat.' So, relieved of responsibility, we groped our way through the graves to the exit.

'You know it isn't a bat,' said my guardian angel, 'but a bird that's fallen through the roof. If you don't go back, I don't know how you'll ever have the face to give that nice sermon again, about caring for God's creatures.'

Well, neither did I – and there was a lot of wear still in that sermon. Sulkily I left the group, got the bird, and in the dark I took the wrong turning. When they finally found me, I was as shaken as the fluttering feathers in my hand.

'Come on, let's visit those de luxe shops on the Via Condotti,' said my guardian angel soothingly. 'You like all that Gucci Pucci stuff.' 'But I can't afford those things.' 'You can enjoy without owning,' said my guardian angel. 'Any angel can teach you that.'

Well, we had a wonderful time window shopping and a polite assistant gave us free squirts of aftershave.

Later on in Santa Maria Maggiore, we sat companionably together, examining the golden angels in the mosaics. 'Stay with me,' I said. 'Where do we go next together? Los Angeles?' he said hopefully. I laughed. Well, I would certainly need a guardian angel there.

Now I don't know whether my guardian angel is fact or phantasy – whether he's a religious reality or something cooked up in my psyche. But do take your own guardian angel along with you on holiday. Whether he'll guard you against pick-pockets and muggers I don't know. But he'll certainly guard you against your own worst enemy – yourself.

## *Bus stop*

I bumped into him by the bus stop outside the psychiatric hospital. He looked lost, as patients do after their discharge. He could go home now – if he had one, which he hadn't, because his wife had had enough and left him. I pieced his story together while we waited.

We were going the same way, so we stopped off at a café, and celebrated his release with beans, bangers and doughnuts. But how was he going to get started in an empty flat, when there was nothing to wake up for?

'Join the club,' I said. 'Lots of people can't get started. Some can't fill in a form. Some can't post a letter. Some can't cope with the washing up and have to eat out.'

In my twenties I couldn't get out of bed. I lay there listening to the letters sliding through the letter box and the ringing phone. It wasn't laziness but fear. They were demands which turned into threats as I delayed.

'Now comes padre's pep talk on the power of prayer,' he said caustically – he was entitled to his feelings. 'Prayer didn't save me,' I said, 'it was the BBC light programme. If I turned it on when I woke up, my world wasn't empty. If I managed to move my body to the rock 'n' roll beat, it shifted my mood too. I used to hokey-cokey round the bedroom and shimmy and shake to the bathroom.'

'Crikey!' he said and I admit a semi-naked rabbi on a rug, cutting a rug, is not a pretty sight, but who cares if you're on your own.

'Give me some more tips,' he said, beginning to enjoy himself. 'Well, I sang. Not hymns, but rugger songs, advertising jingles and Rosenkavalier – all parts. And if I could get down and dressed, I rewarded myself with a tin of cold custard.'

'So God didn't come into it?' he said sardonically, for like many people he was a spiritual snob who couldn't see God in ordinary things like cold custard, only in extraordinary sensational ones.

But religion doesn't need an 'r' in the month, so I told him the story of the rabbi who was marooned in a flood.

First a helicopter hovered over him, but the rabbi gave no signal, for God would find him in His own

'The longest journey begins with a single tin.'

CUSTARD

time. Then a boat passed by, but the rabbi meditated on in silence. The flood waters rose higher, and then the rabbi prayed. 'I wait patiently for your salvation, Lord, how long?' A voice came from heaven. 'I've already sent my salvation twice, you idiot, and you sent it back both times.'

'God redeemed me via the radio, the hokey-cokey and tins of cold custard. Have another doughnut.'

He laughed. 'Will God come to me too?' 'But he already has,' I said, 'and you haven't noticed it – just like the rabbi in the story. God has already used me to make you laugh again.' He was puzzling over this theological conundrum when we parted. For the first time he had forgotten his sorrows.

# *Freddy*

Whenever poor Marcel Proust heard a delicate tune, it reminded him of dainty teas with duchesses. I'm coarser and smells switch my memory on.

I was eating baked beans in a caf, when I smelt a bowl of stew. It took me back to Amsterdam in the fifties, when I lived on mangel-wurzels and bronto-saurus bones.

You may want the following recipe for yourself, but it belongs to my friend Freddy who rescued me when I'd lost everything. I'd arrived late from Germany, to a send-off for a family, sailing across the North Sea. We waved them goodbye, settled down to Dutch gin and herrings, and sang revolutionary songs to annoy the bourgeois beasts above us.

When the party broke up, I found the family had sailed off with my luggage. My toothbrush and travellers cheques were heading in the direction of the Dogger Bank – if that family could find it – they were pretty far gone. I was far gone too and sat on the pavement, and wept, praying the street would stop going round.

A passer-by stopped, shook his head and took me back to his attic in pity. He was very poor and at the weekend raided the market for leftovers – ripe fruit, camemberts on the turn, mammoth bones, and rude looking roots. That night it became goulash, and then a risotto. Finally he curried the remains. Even the hot curry couldn't suppress the taste of true brontosaurus, and the smell of stew still reminds me of my friend Freddy.

Now, I don't share Freddy's taste in food, or politics. He Hoovers the debris; I hide it. We quarrel, sulk, don't speak for months, and then say sorry. We've gone on like that for years. What keeps us together is a mystery!

No sex, no certificate signed by any civil servant or priest binds us together, because there's no special liturgy or service for friends. Which is a pity! The old extended family is breaking down. Clerics and politicians deplore it, and I'm sorry too. But God is not limited by sociology. He's busy creating different sorts of families. Often in a modern city, your new family are your friends.

Like many people, I've had difficulty using the traditional images of God, because they don't fit my situation. God as parent – well, I've spent so much time sorting out that relationship with an analyst, I don't dare project it on to the cosmos. And God as King – the only monarchs I've lived under reign, but don't rule. And lover won't do, because if you mix sex into the sacred, anything can happen. The relationships which help me and you come close to God are those where we care for another creature, or another creature cares for us – whether it's a sympathetic social worker, baby, pet or friend. I've been thinking a lot about God lately. People do before their sixtieth birthday. But when I try to invoke His presence it helps if I think of Him as a friend, just like Freddy.

21

# A floating hell to Belgium

I was arguing with a doctor about a chap who liked bed-hopping, much to the fury of assorted husbands, toyboys and live-in lovers. 'It's just an addiction,' said the doctor. 'The poor chap's trying to run away from something.' 'A shotgun,' I suggested.

'Now don't be hard, Lionel,' said my doctor friend. 'You had a bad enough time getting over your addiction' – a remark which was below the belt because I haven't touched tobacco now for ten years. But I was a teenage addict, and at the age of fourteen I started to smoke two packs a day. I used to wake up retching over my first fag, and fell asleep with one between my lips. My sheets had little rows of burn marks like bullet holes to prove it. And I'm amazed I survived unroasted.

I still remember a dreadful sail to Belgium in a small boat. We found out we'd forgotten the fags, when we were out at sea, and the wind wouldn't blow us back. Well, we tried shredded wheat wrapped in kitchen roll, and mixed herbs in loo paper, lint, cotton wool and lentils. They were so dreadful, I decided to break loose.

As my body got adjusted to nicotine loss, my friends were supportive and understanding about the strange grunts and gurgles which came from it. And when this happened on a pulpit, my congregation just smiled and carried on praying.

Help from above also came from prayer, which is why reformed addicts like me are so often religious. We know it works. But my doctor friend was right. I was only cured when I stopped carrying the burden of other people's expectations, for that had caused the stress which had made me smoke. And I pass on this advice. You don't have to be a success, for the good life is not the same as the smart life. If you prefer a pot of tea and a tin of pilchards to a trendy restaurant, God doesn't mind. It's all right with Him if you want to assemble your wardrobe from charity shops. The prophets didn't buy their loin cloths in boutiques. No one can rat race against you if you decline to race against them.

I got unintentional support from a monastery where I went to lecture. They told me they were the postulant house of their order. But where were the postulants? The monks all looked pretty ancient to me. Well, they hadn't had any for fifteen years. They just carried on, resigned but ready. I could have kissed them because they hadn't sold their souls to success, or pawned them in the numbers game. And if you can do the same, you may not have to smoke, booze or bed-hop.

# *First Steps Abroad*

The excitement of travel hit me when I was very young. Whenever anything nasty made the headlines – Mosley, Hitler or unemployment – I opted out of my surroundings and daydreamed of far-off places like Southend or Margate. I stood silently in the children's playground, enraptured by place names, reciting silently the list of London stations like a litany.

I mixed up holidays with holy days at a very early age, and have never got them separated. When I was five, a kind uncle gave me a book of English poetry, which I loved but hardly understood. It included some lines of Henry Vaughan, which I learnt by heart in bed.

'My soul there is a country far beyond the stars
Where stands a winged sentry all skilful in the
  wars . . .
If thou canst get but thither, there grows the flower
  of peace
The rose that cannot wither, thy fortress and thy
  ease'

Wherever I went in those early days – Southend, Holland, or around England fleeing the Blitz – that was my true destination. It is still!

# *Southend in slow motion*

When I was a kid, for six months of the year I mused, brooded and phantasised about Southend. Southend meant sophistication, stardust and dreams come true. We saved up a whole year for our week away, which always began on August Bank Holiday.

We packed and re-packed a dozen times, and dad sat me on the suitcases while he did up the straps. And then there were frantic letters which went to and fro between us and the boarding house. One more wanted to squeeze in, then it was two. Could they sleep on a camp bed or a sofa? Had the boarding house got our letters? Was it twenty-two bob a week all in, or twenty without high tea? Were we allowed baths and how much extra? Could we return to our rooms during the afternoon?

For months before, our family council was in continual session. I was sick with excitement long before we fought our way to the train, and physically sick when I was on it.

There were no loos or corridors on those trains, so a retching, incontinent kid was a problem which modern travellers have mercifully forgotten. While the rest of the carriage closed their eyes or looked the other way, children were hoisted up to the windows. It was awful if you were a small boy – it was even worse if you were a small girl.

Everybody tried to be so genteel. In the mornings, the ladies sauntered by in beach pyjamas, and in the evening they paraded along the front, wearing dead and grizzly fox furs draped over their bosoms. I loathed their glassy eyes, and revenged myself by dipping their tails in the tea cups, and got my bucket and spade confiscated.

Life was much slower and statelier. You didn't meet and mate in discos. Suitable young men were vetted and allowed to take tea with my mother's youngest sister, with me as the unwanted and unwilling chaperone. They bribed me with bullseyes. I can't remember anyone drunk or going haywire as they do on the Costas today. It was a slow motion world. Holidaymakers sat in little shelters on the prom and sucked chocolate slowly – if they chewed it, it wouldn't last so long. And they stared for a long time at the sea until the gentle silence washed away their bitterness and worries, of which they had lots, because they had a hard life after the slump.

I used to think all this waiting and watching was a waste of time. But it recharged their spirits. People are better off now it's true, but their holidays are spoilt by stress and envy. In the rat race you have to run ever harder to remain in the same place. Well, here's some advice which works just as well in a five star hotel by the Med as in a B and B facing the North Sea.

Remember your soul needs a break as well as your

body. It needs some silence and quiet not more bar-
becues and booze. There's a lot of healing in nature if
you're willing to let it work. It doesn't cost anything –
God's given it for free. So why not find a quiet spot, sit
down, suck some chocolate and watch the waves for
an hour. They'll wash away all your bad vibes and
you'll feel as placid and peaceful as the contented cows
pictured on margarine tubs. It was a simple therapy
that worked in Southend, and it might do the same for
you now.

# Refugee from Protestant prayers

During the war I was evacuated to the country and, at school assemblies, all exotic non-Christians like me had to leave the hall before prayers and wait outside. There was intense speculation among us emigrants as to what went on after we left. Some said the others were taught Protestant passwords, and some that they were given secret rations of sweets because they were established and special.

Well, I've never lost my curiosity about what goes on inside the established church of this country, and I was glued to the TV watching all the Anglican bishops parading into Canterbury Cathedral for their Lambeth Conference, as colourful as peacocks, though not of course as proud. Looking at them I couldn't help thinking of the bishop I'd known best, the late Right Reverend Colin Winter, once Bishop of Damaraland-in-exile. He would have loved the holy razamataz.

I first met him when I was up at Oxford. He was studying theology, and he gave me the shock of my life when he addressed me in market Yiddish. He learnt it when he flogged nylons in Petticoat Lane to help him pay for his theology studies. Colin and I hitchhiked together all over Europe, and he really lived his Christianity. We shared one razor blade, one toothbrush – and one pair of socks.

Through him I found out that Anglicans could laugh at themselves like the Irish and the Jews.

A friend of Colin's who was very very high church, had got sent to a parish which was the lowest of the low. Well, he introduced incense and he explained carefully to a young lorry driver how to use the censer. When he processed in for the service, he saw a cloud of black smoke and sparks belching out of it. 'What is burning?' he intoned in that high and holy Anglican voice. 'The flaming charcoal,' bellowed the server in response. They had to extinguish it with a bucket of water before he could proceed.

'Holy smoke!'

Colin had a breezy way with liturgical upsets and I tried to imitate this holy nonchalance. Once when I was taking a service out of Britain, they had to yank the organist out of a bar. When I entered in procession, hands prayerfully together, and looking down my nose, he played helpfully the 'Entry of the Clowns' for he also worked part time at a circus. It brought down the house, and I felt really mortified, but then I thought of Colin and allowed myself a cackle of laughter.

Colin also showed me the caring side of the C of E as well as its comedy and I owe him and it a big debt.

There's the club for down and outs in a church crypt in Aldgate, where the vicar and his helpers do the serving, waiting and washing up. Both you and I could fall through a black hole in the social system, and thank God for such a club.

It was there I first met the Anglican Franciscans who survive on air and baked beans. They seem to have a motto 'If it's human, hug it'.

Well, an Anglican nun certainly hugged me once. I came to her convent to give a lecture. She took one look at me, put her arms around me and said 'You poor dear!' I promptly burst into tears because I was over-working, and so grateful she noticed.

There're Anglican midwives too, whose strong language and soft hearts are a joy.

If you're an 'insider' religious professional, documents, definitions and conference resolutions matter a lot. But for an outsider it's only the caring and kindness that remain with you. That's why I still remember my friend Colin after so many years.

# Dutch treat

I first went abroad when the war ended. My parents sent me to Holland because it seemed a safe sort of place. I would stare at clogs and cows and drool over Delft in clean country air. But I had had enough clean country air during the evacuation, and what I wanted was city dust and dance halls. My mind was full of passion, my face full of pimples, and I longed for love.

Rotterdam was still a ruin, so I pressed on to Amsterdam, where I promptly fell ill with fever, became delirious and found myself in an empty student flat in the city centre with some lovely ladies who lived below, and who cluck-clucked over my plight. I only learnt about their livelihood later when I told a family friend who winked and said he wouldn't split on me.

Above me in the attic slept a student who had two female friends, who visited at different times. At least that was the theory of it, but it didn't happen that way and when it didn't, all three got excited and declaimed in Dutch and threw things and that's how a book of Dutch love poetry landed in my lap.

Feverish and forlorn I brooded over my situation. The house was full of love, I could hear it going on above me and below me, and I was just the dull filling in an exciting sex sandwich.

But on my bed of pain I learnt some important lessons about sex and love and the difference between them. I saw that sex on its own was obsessive. It could make the serious student above me rather silly and the kind ladies below me inconsistent. Sometimes they all brought me buckets of soup, and sometimes they forgot all about me and let me starve. Concentration on sex didn't exactly make them selfish but it did make them self-centred.

I learnt about the love I could rely on from the rough hands of the ageing charwoman who did for me, dosed me and held me in her arms when I shook with fever. I used to watch as she slurped suds around my bed. I once wondered who paid her while I was ill, because I didn't. Probably no one. But I never thought it through, because I was too preoccupied with my own sadness.

I just hoped that God's hands would hold me like hers, if it was time for me to leave this life. I told this to her and she gave me a look of such pity I burst into tears. She then clasped me to her vast bosom. I still remember the clean, soapy smell of her – and asked me if I'd like a kiss to cheer me up. Wouldn't I just! Frantically I peeked through my Dutch dictionary, because I was pedantic as well as pimply. 'Ach ja, mevrouw,' I croaked, groaning Dutch gutterals through my inflamed tonsils 'erg graag' – 'if you don't mind.' It wasn't anything at all like the love I'd longed for but it meant much more than the goings-on below me or the high passion above me. It was the real thing, and for the moment I was content.

# Home from home

In 1940 an invasion was expected hourly. My parents brought me back to London from the country, and each night we slept in the vaults of a brewery in the Mile End Road. After the morning all clear, we packed up our bedding, and hurried back home to see if we still had one.

One day we came back and it wasn't there – just a smoking hole instead. My mother found a barrow and we loaded on to it the remnants, a bakelite Ecko radio with its bottom blown off and a dud shell that dad turned into a cigarette lighter. My father wheeled the barrow to the lockup for bombed out people like us and that was that.

I never trusted again in the permanence of homes made of solid things like bricks, mortar and mortgages. When you've seen one home blown up, you don't believe in the rest. This distrust is confirmed as I drop into charity shops on my way to work, and sift through the debris of other people's hopes and homes.

During a wandering life, I've learnt how to make my home in hotels, hospitals, boarding houses and bedsits instead. It's useful knowledge and I'll tell you how it's done, because you may have reserved a room in a high rise hotel for your holiday this summer on some crowded Costa. It sounded beautiful in the brochure but when you let yourself into it, it's so blank and bright and un-homey you want to rush out to the nearest bar or bistro to find something familiar and friendly.

Well, why not make friends with the room first! Don't unpack, just potter. Pretend you're an artist and consider its light and shade and shadows. Don't turn on the radio, risk the room's silence. Sit still in it, let the silence surround you, and suck you into itself. But you're worried if the tap will drip, or the blind will get stuck. The only thing worth worrying about is worrying. You can't complain to the management just because your room's pleasant not perfect.

Instead, make friends with yourself as well as the room, because home is in you not just your hotel. The walls you resent are only mirrors reflecting back your own restlessness. Let the silence of your room swallow up your faults and failures and its emptiness purify you.

Now it's time to make friends with God. And this is how you do it. Relax, open your hands and lay them palm upwards on your knees and ask God in to be your guest. When His still small voice starts to sing in the silence, close your eyes. When they open in their own time, your blank, bright room will seem more kind and cosy.

Now you're ready to saunter down for a drink in the hotel bar, confident because you've got a home to return to, not just a room. And you may remember some old familiar words as you sip your sangria, 'And God saw all He had created and behold it was very good.'

# A Package to Paradise

I am not a wealthy person, but I too long for film star luxury. The nearest I ever get to it is on a package.

Two star and three star hotels have marble foyers, lined with uncomfortable, luxurious-looking chairs, all illuminated with a real sparkler of a chandelier.

What does it matter, if too many guests are racing upstairs for too few lifts, or if it's a rugger scrum round the self service buffet? Packages are wonderful value, and all that marble is balm for the ego. Having been used to chilly boarding houses in childhood, when you weren't allowed to go back in the afternoon, I can only say 'My, my!' as I pretend to dress for dinner by putting on a tie, and then saunter down to the nearest bar for a coñac, or konjak or xampañ.

But when I have had my share of glitz and glamour, I want something else. If you bother to seek them out, because they won't come to you, there's usually a hermitage or holy man close by your package paradise, though they are not mentioned in the brochures.

# Castles in Spain

Don't carry unnecessary hand luggage when you go on holiday. I did, my bag burst open and I ran around the airport retrieving toiletries too embarrassing to mention. Suddenly, I remembered arriving at that same airport years before and I was overwhelmed. I had suffered from love and the loss of it ruined my holiday, and I wondered if the memory would rot up this one too. For I'd booked in for a fortnight in Benidorm, a town which makes sophisticates snigger. But they malign it. Benidorm has wide, well-kept streets with palm trees and if there's something in the air, it's only hamburger. And at night, high rise hotel towers twinkle with lights, against the back-drop of wild Spanish sierras, and the beaches are floodlit.

I could imagine Clark Gable there, breathing heavily over some moaning blonde and croaking 'you've got starlight in your eyes, babe, and moonlight in your hair'.

Well, Benidorm doesn't please everybody of course. It was reported that when the American fleet arrived, the lads were told this was the fun city of Europe and they couldn't wait to get at those common, Common-Market chicks in all that glitz and glitter. Now, there is a time and season for all things, says Ecclesiastes in the Bible, but the lads couldn't have read it because they arrived in the wrong season, the low, not the high. So all they found were British oldies like me, dancing foxtrots with blue-rinsed matrons, which came as a shock, and the fleet steamed off in a huff up the Med. I, on the other hand, am grateful to Benidorm, because it has no past and doesn't want any, which stopped me moping.

Rather than use an old castle for their mock medieval jousts, they built a brand new one, made of plastic and concrete, where you can munch pizza while you watch knights every night, to the sound of piped music which prevents any medieval melancholy.

A Scottish lady I met went on a tour to see the real castles nearby, of which there is an abundance, and I'll try to report her words. 'Well,' she said, 'those Moors marauded the Christians and the Christians mutilated the Moors, and they poured frying oil over each other. It doesn't bear thinking about, Rabbi. Give me a tango tea in Benidorm every time.' We went to one and I watched Arabs, Jews, Germans and Spaniards dancing amicably together and not letting their past poison their present.

The Benidormians weren't so wrong. The past is too dead to do much about, and the future, if it exists, is only a glint in God's eyes, but the present is precious and holy, because you can change it and use it to do good to yourself and others.

Holidays are good times to sort out accumulated

litter, the litter in your drawers and the litter in your life. Some bad memories have value because you can learn from them. Some, you can do something about, but a lot of bad memories you won't be able to do anything about, so get rid of those which make you morose and nasty. Dump them on God, they're safe with Him. There's no need, you know, to carry unnecessary luggage in your memories or in your mind, or hands, as you journey through life.

## Singles beware!

Some are searching the shops for bottles of Beaujolais Nouveau. I'm searching the travel bureaux for their new crop of holiday brochures. I sit in the kitchen and consider my strategy for the summer. You get what you pay for in this world – though hopefully not in the next, which means more sun costs more money. But if you're single, places aren't as important as people. Do you risk it alone, or ring round for a friend who doesn't snore?

I can certainly find a couple, because lots of bored couples like a single to string along. But be wary if you're their third leg. Couples can be quite ruthless and you're caught in a pincer movement. 'I say Lionel, old chap, could you leave a bit more butter for Mildred at breakfast. She doesn't like to say so, she's too sensitive but . . .' or, 'Lionel dear, you know how much you mean to my husband. Now I know you

don't want to visit that monastery of flagellating friars
– I can't say I fancy it myself. But it would give George
such pleasure!'

I shudder and decide it's another single or nothing.
But if it's nothing, you risk two weeks of trappist
silence and the table by the kitchen door to punish you
for being partnerless. Also some things are best done
by two, and I don't mean sex. You can't sunoil your
own back. Paella comes in double portions and plonk
in generous jugs or mean single measures. A partner
can also defend your deck chair by the pool. Even
more, you need someone to complain to, and even
more than this, someone to complain about.

I sip my tea and wonder why holiday friendships
don't work for me. The crisis occurs on the third or
fourth day. We sit down for supper, amicably discuss-
ing the weather. We may wonder what the weather's
like in the Falklands, about which we differ. Suddenly

I feel unloved and unwanted and watch helplessly as scenarios from my past overwhelm the present. I sulk, and walk away in a huff. My friend who has to pay the bill is speechless with anger, which makes me feel very sorry for myself.

But if I can find some place of worship and sit in silence, the self pity voices fade away, and another voice starts to speak in me. 'The past is My property,' it says, 'the present is yours. Why ruin its happiness and holiness! Make a mess of your own holiday if that's what you want, but not his.'

I return to the hotel and say sorry. My friend grins and gives me a record as a peace offering. I blush as I read the label. It's 'As Time Goes By'. Play it again Sam!

I say all this with feeling, because holidays are times when expectations run high, which is the reason why there are so many rows. Now we've all got our favourite hurt feelings. Try to forget them! Don't fall for those silly old B Movies whirring round and round and round in your mind.


# *The birds in Torremolinos*

It was absurd! On the Costa del Sol in the height of summer, I was feverish with flu. At first I was confined to my hotel room, but later I was let out on the balcony, where I read the Bible, the only book the hotel could provide, and contemplated the long line of luxury hotels and crumbling concrete which slopes away from Torremolinos to Marbella where the money is. It isn't my favourite Costa, but then it doesn't cost a lot.

I felt fragile but content on my balcony. There was a table with two chairs, some shade to cool my bottles, and like a box at the opera it overlooked Carihuela beach, where it all happens – 'it' being sex. One evening I watched the performers below. Their colour ranged from agony red to painful pink. Golly, I thought, how do they do it? If anyone touched me I'd hit the roof. But no-one did, and I went to bed.

Next morning I stopped reading the Second Book of Samuel while I was munching croissants and peered down at them. The beach was littered with bottles, and the embers of fires still glowed. But there was no glow of love left in the revellers. The girls sat sulkily on one side and their boyfriends looked mean and uncertain on the other.

In my feverish state, I imagined my balcony as a pulpit. St Francis had preached to the birds. Well, I would preach to the birds below and their boyfriends. I leant over and addressed them as follows.

Dear birds and boyfriends. I am not going to burden you with my own morality. My life has not been so holy that I can pontificate over yours. So I shall turn to the Bible and take as my text, the Second Book of Samuel, starting at chapter 13 verse one. I shall read the lesson summary aloud, as you may not have brought your Bibles to the beach.

'Absalom, the son of David, had a fair sister, named Tamar, and Amnon, the son of David, loved her. And he pretended to be sick, and said let my sister come to my bed and feed me cakes. And when she brought them, he was too strong for her, and forced her and lay with her. And then he hated her with more hatred than the love with which he had loved her.'

The psychology and the message of this story still rings true. Never do anything the night before which makes you hate or despise your partner or yourself the next morning. It is very basic but very true, and much morality is based on it.

So endeth my sermon to the birds and their boy-friends.

On the beach, the birds scarcely noticed me – but a boyfriend did, and he heaved a bottle half heartedly in my direction. I moved inside smartly, before he could hurl anything else. St Francis got better treatment from his birds, but that's the difference between life and legend, isn't it?

# *Marbella (where the money is!)*

Today I want to warn you, not about the sufferings life inflicts on us, but the unhappiness we inflict on ourselves.

On the Costa del Sol, my fever had gone, and I joined the holiday makers by the beach. Large blonde ladies overflowed their bikinis, girls from Bradford plotted to capture a José or Jaime. Holiday home touts promised the freehold of Paradise, and an old man of ninety sashayed along, held up by his truss.

I suddenly thought I recognised someone there, an acquaintance not a friend. I recognised his neighing, braying laugh.

Puzzled, I turned to examine the coach trips on offer. One promised the fountains of Granada. Another the cathedral at Cordoba. And another said 'Come to Marbella – Where the Money Is'. What was it like to be wealthy? I was curious. So was an OAP called Doris, and we went on together.

As we neared Marbella our guide inflamed us with its marvels. 'Be careful in cafés – the prices!' He pursed his lips and pressed his finger tips together. We narrowed our eyes and nodded. 'Greenbacks, gelt, the old payola.'

But this made Doris bolshie. 'Don't worry Rabbi – I'll save up for a down payment on two cuppas.' The guide glared and pointed to a blank wall. 'A famous celebrity lives here,' he hissed. 'What's she famous for?' said Doris. 'She's famous for being a celebrity.' 'I bet they're all bank robbers,' said Doris disparagingly.

There was indeed more marble in Marbella – and more credit companies. But in the café Doris was despondent. 'Why, they're no different from us.'

Again I heard the neighing, braying laugh and recognised the Tempter. The Costa was his sort of place. Don't the rabbis say 'The Tempter goes about the world, thrusting his closed fist before people's faces. Guess what's in it, he taunts them. And people think it's what they want most, and die to get it. Then

48

'It's odd. I didn't like you much at home but I can't stand the sight of you out here.'

the Tempter opens his fist and laughs, for there's nothing there.'

I listened to the conversations at tables around me. 'We didn't get on in London, but it'll be different in our holiday home – I know it.'

'Yes, he's called Hosey. He works as a waiter, but he's a film producer really, and he'll wait for me till I come back next Christmas.'

'If only I had a room on the fourth floor, I would be really happy.'

The Tempter was having a field day. I wanted to warn them with another text, but didn't.

People long for things that cannot help them, and are frightened of things that cannot hurt them – for it is something inside themselves they're afraid of, and something inside themselves they long for.

# Life is a Moving Staircase

Even if we stand still in space, we journey through time. Life is an escalator like those in stores and underground stations. We move on, though we do nothing.

The same things surround us, but we see them always from new perspectives. I live once again with my mother and aunt in a suburban house – we were in the same situation fifty years ago. But now our roles are reversed, and I am the caring adult. There is a lot to think about.

There is a lot to ponder in the fabric of ordinary life, in the familiar, routine, and unremarkable happenings of an ordinary day. At first I was too romantic and snobbish to see it. Now, I know I do not only have to read scriptures, I also have to decipher the scripture that is unfolding around me.

# 'Mink Schmink!'

I sulk over my supper because some of my savings have been 'corrected' on the stock exchange. 'Put not your trust in princes,' says the Bible. Well, in future I won't. I'll put it in a building society instead.

My aunt tries to cheer me up as she used to when I was a child.

'Knock, knock,' she says brightly.
'Who's there?' I answer obediently.
'Arthur.'
'Arthur who?'

'O Lionel!' she whispers, 'I can't remember', and she passes a trembling hand over her face, the way elderly people do. I try to comfort her but she thrusts her post office savings book at me – 'It's yours dear,' she says passionately. 'I'd give my right arm and leg for you.' I tell her, tactfully, I need neither.

My mother meanwhile has been poking about in a cupboard and pulls out a plastic bag. 'Here's your inheritance,' she exclaims. My inheritance smells of moth balls – it's my mother's mink.

Nobody bought it for her she says. She saved up for it herself – penny by penny. She can't wear it now of course, because she seems to have got smaller and the mink bigger, and she hasn't the strength to support it. Ma says it makes her look like Bond Street. But I don't care for fur, and it reminds me of *Watership Down*. My aunt looks at it wistfully and says Mink Schmink.

I thank my mother and go to bed. But before I can get to sleep, there's a tap at the door and my aunt peers in. 'I've remembered it Lionel,' she says proudly.

'Knock, knock.'
'Who's there?'
'Arthur.'
'Arthur who?'
'Ar-ther mometer.'

I laugh, and my aunt goes out gratified.

I am just about to turn off the radio and try to go to sleep again when I sit up shocked. I hear about a bomb that has exploded in Ireland, and that innocent people have been murdered. Suddenly, I'm ashamed of my sulks and little losses and try to think of the real things in life. I remember Remembrance Day will soon be with us. I've a lot to remember.

Lying in bed I remember the families of those who died in Ireland and pray for them. I remember, for the first time in years, nice neighbours who were blown up in the Blitz. I remember dimly a boy I used to play with of my age. Why did he go, not me? I remember I'm the first generation in my family that hasn't had to fight in a world war. I remember how lucky I am I was born in Britain. I remember my mother's cousins who were not so lucky and got gassed in concentration camps – there were worse ways too!

What they would have given to be alive and enjoy my losses! I hear my mother and aunt going to bed downstairs and remember the real treasures of life, two elderly ladies who don't hurt anyone and who love me to their last penny and pelt.

# My secretary

About fifteen years ago I needed a new secretary. My organisation advertised and engaged a friendly, pleasant lady of my own generation. I wondered how we would get on, for we had to share an office, and we would be closer to each other than to our own families, and for longer hours.

Well, we got on so well, I wondered if I knew her and sometimes I saw she eyed me speculatively over her typewriter.

Then one day, I dictated my CV to her. 'I was born,' I dictated, 'in the East End of London near White-chapel.' Suddenly we looked at each other and knew. We had last seen each other in 1936, when we lived opposite each other in a little street behind London Hospital. Both our families had faced hard times in the depression. I went to school with her little sister, and my secretary was allowed to help bath me if she was good.

Then my father became a factory foreman and we moved into a whole house several streets away. We never saw each other again – till now that is.

For a while we were overwhelmed with memories but the phone rang and we had to get back to work. Together we administrate a small office for the Reform Jewish community, dealing with the things which according to the book ought not to have happened – when a Christian lad falls in love with the Jewish girl over the garden fence, and it's a case of Goy meets girl and a religious mess. Or when a couple separate after their children have left home, because all that kept them together has gone.

The Bible tells us God's word to priests, seers and soldiers. But what is the word of God to people like us, secretaries, pen-pushers, and petty bureaucrats?

God tells us to give cups of coffee to our clients. People in trouble are dear to Him and need cosseting.

God tells us to try and treat them as individuals, not as types or troublemakers. The Nazis saw the Jews as types, so they never saw the real flesh and blood and feeling before them – which is why they could kill!

God also tells me to say 'maybe' when I want to say 'no' because 'no' would be much easier. 'No' means end of problem and 'maybe' means more work for me. Lots of people prefer 'no' because they think religion is like medicine. It isn't real unless it's nasty.

God tells us to let ourselves be taken for a ride occasionally – though not to be door mats, because that doesn't help anybody. The problem for religious professionals is not sex as many people think but power.

Some people of course you can't help.

There was this lady who said to her lawyer, 'My marriage is a mystery, but I'll get to the bottom of it.'

'What happened?' he asked.

'Well this man knocks at my door and asks "Lady, is your husband at home?" "No," I say, "my husband is a hard worker who leaves home at eight and comes back at six in the evening." He then pushes the door open and embraces me!'

'So?' said her lawyer.

'Well, the same guy comes around the next week, knocks at the door and asks "Madam, is your husband at home?" "No," I say "I told you last time, he's a hard worker who leaves home at eight and comes back at six." He pushes the door open and embraces me again. It's a mystery and I'm going to get to the bottom of it.'

'What's the mystery?' asked the bemused lawyer. She pursed her lips. 'So what's his business with my husband?'

As my secretary so rightly says, 'And the band played "Believe It If You Can" Lionel!'

# The art of failure

If you have ever been to a Jewish wedding, you will know that the bride and bridegroom drink twice from a chalice of wine. An old rabbi once told me they drink twice because the wine represents both the good times and the bad times they'll share together, joy and sorrow, success and failure.

Although it's wine, it stands for the cocktail of life – all the experiences, nice and nasty, they need to make a real marriage.

Now many people find failure difficult. They want to disown it, or hide it or say it belongs to someone else. Some people don't even like going near failures, because they think it might be catching, and some of the failure will rub off on them.

But failure like success is part of life. It's something God meant us to go through, because we can't grow up without it. After all, all of us are failures when we die.

Now I know being a failure is difficult so here are some tips to lighten the load.

Ask yourself 'failure or success – in whose eyes?' God might have a very different view from you about which is which.

In my life I've sat through more services than I can remember, but the one I've never forgotten was a failure. I'd just missed a train and having nothing better to do I wandered into a Quaker meeting down the road. An old man pushed past me at the door and commandeered a seat in the front row.

The chairman of the meeting said a short prayer, asking the Holy Spirit to prompt us, and he didn't have long to wait. The old boy promptly jumped up, and launched into a tirade about all the people who had defrauded him, done him down and generally got on his goat. He was querulous, cantankerous and boring as self-centred people usually are.

Was anyone going to stop him? Apparently not! The congregation sat with closed eyes in prayerful silence, meditating respectfully on his nonsense. Well, he went on for forty minutes and at the end, people opened their eyes, smiled at him and shook his hand. The chairman greeted him courteously and thanked him for his message, and they all filed sedately into the street, the old boy still mumbling away over his wrongs.

That service was a failure, but it moved me more than the finest liturgy. The religion wasn't in the words – it was in the politeness of the people. I've never known a service where God was so present.

Also remember if you're a failure that you're in good company – the best! Moses never set foot in the Promised Land he longed for, and most people thought Jesus was a failure after he was arrested.

On a less exalted level, Groucho Marx failed to get into an exclusive country club where Jews weren't allowed to bathe. 'I'll tell you what,' he said, 'my son is only half Jewish, so can he get wet up to his waist?'

If it's your turn to fail, don't despise yourself. Accept it, learn from it, laugh at it, and then forget it. Don't take it personally. 'That's life!'

# Teach yourself to be a sage

I was a serious youngster who wanted to learn about life. Somewhere there must be a teacher who could tell it all. I couldn't afford to go to a guru in India or get turned on by a red hot evangelist in the States, so I dropped into chilly clubs and church halls instead, and carefully considered the courses of salvation on offer, both individual and universal.

Sitting solidly in the middle seats of the middle row, with a tube of peppermints, I was preached at by assorted priests, prophets, sages and seers. Some gave away biscuits and some just good advice. I tried to be impartial, showing neither fear nor favour, but a free bun did make me less judgmental.

My quest ended in a small, sparsely attended hall. The subject was bliss, but the sage spoke so sadly, I decided to make my getaway, and tiptoed softly down the aisle to the door. But the speaker stopped suddenly in mid-sentence, and pointing a beseeching finger at me cried out, 'Don't go now sir, it gets better as it goes along.' I swallowed my peppermints in surprise and sat down abruptly, and a bearded gentleman beamed benevolently at me. I was shocked. How could a Teacher beseech a learner like me? It was against the rules!

Well, the talk did get a bit better, because the speaker began to behead blossoms – 'like the Buddha' he said and I'd never seen that done before.

On top of the bus going home I brooded over my new knowledge. Since even saviours depended on someone to save them, then all of us can be saviours, and together we save each other. There was no need to go to any more meetings. I had found the saviour I sought – some of him was inside me.

But if you do go on a guru hunt keep your common

sense. Trust teachers who care for their own souls and other people's bodies. Be cautious about teachers who care for their own bodies, and other people's souls.

Also don't believe people who promise too much – that you can change yourself on the cheap, or that you don't have to change yourself, just others, or that you can change the universe to suit your convenience.

Consider the case of a trusting friend of mine. His business had gone bankrupt and his wife had left him, and he was thinking of ending it all on a bridge over the river. Suddenly he saw a ragged old woman watching him from under a lamppost. 'I wouldn't do that,' she said.

'What business is it of yours?' he answered bitterly. 'I'm a good fairy,' she answered quietly, 'and I can give you two wishes.'

'You mean I could get my wife back and my business back,' stammered my friend, excited in spite of himself. 'Sure,' she said, 'we fairies require no favours, only a loving embrace from a human being.'

Overcome by gratitude, my friend took her in his arms and embraced her. When he released her, the old woman gazed at him dreamily. 'How old are you?' she asked. 'Forty-two.' 'Hm . . . forty-two and still believes in fairies!' Well, you've been warned!

# *Thoughts on coming closer to a British Rail Senior Citizen card*

The disadvantages of growing old are obvious and I do not want to minimise them – the main one being that your body begins to pack up and like any old engine needs a medical MOT. But until they find out how to slow down the ageing process (which might be quite soon), it is worthwhile considering some of the plusses and puzzles which appear in your late fifties.

Firstly, you are relieved from the burden of expectation, which in Jewish life especially, is a heavy one. It is put on our back in babyhood. God help the Jewish child who dares to be dim and not dyslexic. Approaching your sixties your achievement, whatever it is, is banked and the rest is, so to speak, 'gravy'. This is a relief, and certainly makes me a little fancy-free, though not really rapturous.

In old master paintings of elderly people, the outer shell of flesh seems thin and see through, so the inner light of personality and soul seems correspondingly stronger. I think my inner life is rightly becoming more important to me, because the horizon has come closer, and sensible reality seems less solid than it did – perhaps because the instinctive drives of sex and success are less bothersome. The world and all human achievement will of course end for all of us sometime and hopefully return to whatever it preceded from. What used to be threatening is now comforting.

You can't help getting stuck in the jargon of your past. My mother for example calls all modern design 'futurist'. I must be stuck too, though I do not spot it. I am for example astonished by the use of such current religious 'in' words as 'identity' or 'authenticity', which seem bizarre and rather creepy. Surely you find your identity within you – not in the ideologies or rituals around you. And what is the difference between modern 'authenticity' and old style 'integrity'?

There is a feeling of freedom once again, and I do not mean the right to go on a cheap day excursion to Aberdeen in November – the feeling that you have earned the right to state the truth, your own truth, without aggression. You have also begun to understand what this truth is, and it is certainly not pretending to be the pious old person younger people like you to be, swathed in ritualia, the standard stuff of Jewish pious illustrations. You know too much to fall for that type-casting.

If you're lucky, you've learnt once again the basic arts which make life a lot smoother for you and everybody else.

You can admit you've made a mistake (lots of them). You don't have to bluff them out. You don't have to feel dreadful if you dislike someone – though it's not polite to show it. You know that people have the right to make their own mistakes (if they are mistakes) and you are not God's gestapo, sent to bully them into your conformity.

On reading back this wisdom, I feel a bit bogus. It is self-gratification to play Old Father Time when you are not yet sixty, and entitled to that magic card. Still, like the spies Moses sent ahead to report on the Promised Land, it is advisable to search out life's landscape before you get there and ponder what will happen in the next ten years (or less).

One thing I have realised will not happen, which I used to be fairly certain would happen – is that my religious puzzles, problems and doubts will not be resolved by more knowledge or research. Possibly a little by religious experience, though that is unpredictable. The horizon after all never comes nearer, it always recedes before you. But it doesn't matter, because there's always just enough religion for the next step ahead. Lots of people want religion to give them roots, to make them feel secure. But security is not on offer, only courage and hope to face the unfamiliar.

# 'To Be A Pilgrim'

I sometimes take a bus or a suburban train, and return to a house or flat I lived in long ago. I wasn't particularly happy there, and there is no one left I know. But I want to stare for a few minutes – because that house or flat has something to say to me. I need to lay the ghosts to rest. When I return I feel quieter and cleaner in spirit.

It was only an ordinary house or flat which was my place of private pilgrimage.

I go of course to more recognised places of pilgrimage too, though up to now I have never visited the great Christian pilgrimage centres such as Lourdes or Fatima or the Jewish ones at Safed or the Wailing Wall. I suppose I prefer more intimate shrines. I visit Kings Lynn, because I like that holy crackpot Margery Kempe. She wasn't quite a first class mystic so we have a lot in common. I also look up at the window of good women in Liverpool Cathedral, and this year I shall go to Bedford, Bunyan's birthplace.

Pilgrimage is important to me, and is the reason for many of my journeys. I travel across the years, centuries sometimes and contact people who have some lesson for me, though it takes me years to work out what it is.

# To a ruined synagogue

I often go to Berlin – officially for conferences, unofficially to see my old friend, a German pastor I call
White Rabbit, because he's so busy doing good,
he's always late, like the white rabbit in *Alice in
Wonderland*.

I first met him years ago in London. He burst into
my office and asked me to unbaptise a hundred Jews. I
thought he was dotty. Then he told me his story.
During the war he baptised every Jew he could find to
delay their round up. He didn't want to take any
religious advantage, that's all.

After a conference we slip away on a private pilgrimage. There are some thoughts we only want to think in
each other's company.

White Rabbit drives us past a pretty suburban
station. That's where they deported some of the last
Jews in Berlin – including grandpas and grannies.
They pushed them into trucks at night . . . but it's
better not to think about the details.

We stop at the traffic lights near the old Anhalt
station. There's a big empty space near there which I
don't look at. It's where the gestapo interrogated their

victims, but it's better not to think about that either. You play hide and seek with ghosts in Berlin.

We wait in a queue of cars to cross to the east at Checkpoint Charlie. We don't go with the traffic down Karl Marx Allee but turn off to a shabby part of the town. There it is, a gaunt synagogue, still in ruins, just as the Nazis left it, when they burnt it down on November 9th 1938. We sit in the car and stare at it in silence, thinking of people we knew. Who is he thinking of? Perhaps of his teacher Bonhoeffer, whom they executed just before the end of war. Perhaps of people only he remembers. There are many like that.

I remember a lady without a name, who used to sit on her own in the synagogue, near my mother. She was the German wife of a Jewish chap. They emigrated, she converted, he died and she was stranded here without family or friends. She was 'treu', a German word for faithful. Would I have been so treu? God alone knows!

I think of Albert, my fellow rabbi and friend. On November 9th he had hopped from train to train with his father throughout the night to avoid capture. The gestapo were sitting in their kitchen. I think of another friend whose father was caught and never recovered.

Then I think of a German man, a nice chap, I hadn't seen for years. He tried to put out the flames, got arrested, lost his job, and then was in the Nazi army. Hitler seemed unbeatable so what was the use!

'Let's get going, White Rabbit,' I tell him, 'I've had enough of the past.' I can't help looking back at the burnt-out building through the rear window.

White Rabbit takes me to a cheerful café in the

Kurfurstendamm, and orders coffee and cream cakes. I brood over how they could have done such things to innocent people. Some say it was the lost war which did it. Some say the slump. Some say it was the radio – because without it Hitler couldn't have hypnotised a nation.

Suddenly I imagine it was my granny who'd been taken away, or my father. I almost choke on my own anger and to relieve my feelings bark at an old waiter who is trying to clear away the dirty cups. White Rabbit looks at me reproachfully. I usually behave better than that.

My God, I think, that's how they must have barked at the old people as they piled them into trucks.

Some people say Hitler's dead. I'm not so sure. There's a little bit of him alive and well in me. Is he alive and well in you?

# *To a memorial in Finchley*

Is there hope in South Africa (now you see it, now you don't!); no stop to slaughter in the Middle East; should women wear mitres? These are problems of the great world, but I want to tell you about a small world – the suburb where I live.

Now, I never used to like suburban life. The tedium of it bored me silly. To mark my rejection, I wore open-necked shirts, refused to go ballroom dancing because the boy led the girl, and criticised my parents for being bourgeois. As soon as I learnt how to hitch-hike, I shook the suburban dust off my feet and only returned for a good feed. But life has brought me full circle, because I now live in the same sort of suburb I left behind.

Finchley is strung out on the roads which run out of London to the North. A naked lady with a sword guards its exits and its entrances. Coming from Golders Green, you've arrived when you spot the gleam on her bronze buttocks. Coming from the north, she rears up at you in full frontal. But the respectable can't remove her, because she's a war memorial to the lads who died in two world wars. She is what they dreamt of. Now, only an old lady and I sometimes pause to remember the sacrifices she stands for.

Suburban life has scarcely changed since I left it. On Sunday, only prayer or pizzas are on offer. If someone talks heatedly about red China, the revolution hasn't arrived, only a new line in dinner-ware. But I've changed because I like it now, and see goodness around me I never noticed before. The front gardens for example, and the disturbing smell of their roses which lingers all the way to the underground. Their owners never sit in them, so they work for the pleasure of passers-by like me, which is very unselfish. In the High Street as one charity shop closes, two spring up in its place, even more charitable, selling weirder household fall-out.

Lovely ladies serve in them, who take as much trouble fitting out a tramp in a 50p suit as they would a 500 guinea one in Saville Row. Brits, Bengalis, Indians East and West, Japanese, Jews and Bahais live peaceful lives in parallel. A neighbour who travels to the Gulf and Tokyo tells me he dreams of our suburban gentility when he's marooned in high rise, high security hotels.

Only one doubt disturbs my suburban content – how deep does our middle class niceness go? A black memorial to the holocaust in a garden silently questions Jew and Gentile alike, for no one knows who the next scapegoat will be. 'You're nice now,' says the black memorial, 'when the price of your house goes ever higher. But what will happen when your little boom goes bust? There were leafy suburbs like yours in Berlin too, whose niceness was not enough.'

I sit and stare at the black memorial and try to be positive and cheerful. Perhaps being British we're more tolerant. I hope so – I begin to pray with fervour.

# *To Norwich*

My mother's father left me no money – just good advice. 'Life isn't fair, boy,' he said, 'but make the best of it.' He did precisely that and courted a succession of buxom cooks, because he liked wine, women and rich food. He lived till ninety, and urged me on his deathbed to turn everything into a treat. 'You'd be a fool not to, boy,' he said, sipped some watered whisky and passed peacefully away.

So I won't give 'Whither Britain?' another workover, I'll tell you instead how to turn Britain into a treat.

Treats for me mean trips and holidays, so here are some suggestions for mini ones, suitable even if you're at the bottom of the list of budget beneficiaries, and possible, even, if you're off it, on supplementary.

What about taking a trip to your city centre with a pack of pies. Distribute them to the derelicts and winos huddled in the doorways. It might be a treat for them, it will certainly be a treat for you, for giving is the greatest pleasure of all, which is why I've put this trip first.

But as April is near, when Chaucer's pilgrims were wending their way to Canterbury, what about a mini pilgrimage? Buy some sandwiches and a train ticket and wend your way to places that meant a lot to you. Sit on a nearby bench and muse as you munch. If you make peace with your past, you'll forgive yourself as well as your enemies, which will make you nicer to live with.

God told Abraham to take a trip from his father's house, and it's important not just to get out of your ghetto physically but also mentally. Otherwise your God will degenerate into a grisly totem that helps mobs of people to murder. So hop on a local bus, and jump off when the area feels unfamiliar. I did and wandered into an African Pentecostal chapel. Two large, beaming ladies sat me between them, and took me through the service. I hadn't felt so swaddled since granny died. At the end they gave me a hug of peace and pumpkin pie, and told me I would see the light.

You can also broaden your religious horizons by a trip to a museum for enlightenment as well as for culture.

Sit before a Buddha and work out what he's smiling at. You can munch a mango while you absorb his benevolence. You don't need the fare to Tibet to find his truth.

Which trip for me? Well I'm off to Norwich to find a lady I found in a footnote long ago at Oxford. Her name was Julian. She lived five hundred years ago. I'll take some mead along to help me feel medieval. Like Dante she took a mystical mini holiday to heaven and hell. When she got back, unlike him, she reported hell was empty, there wasn't even a Jew there, which I appreciate. As my grandpa said, 'If a horse drops from heaven, boy, don't examine its teeth.'

# To my father's grave

I had given sermons at services for thirty-five years, and I desperately needed a break. So instead of thinking up sermons, I bought an English paperback Bible instead and sat on a sunny bench in a cemetery, reading it right through; the naughty and the nasty bits as well as the nice ones.

The English was more prim than the Hebrew original. Take the Joseph story, when Pharoah calls to the captain of the guard. Well, in Hebrew he calls to the head butcher, which shows what the writer thought about the military.

And in the Song of Songs, when the lover describes his beloved, he starts at her top and works his way downward. En route he pays some curious compliments to her navel. But was it her navel? The Hebrew word is unclear and I don't think it's her navel he meant.

But what worried me was the command in Deuteronomy about being perfect which isn't practical or proper because perfection belongs to God not us. It's dangerous advice.

Perfection stops people finishing the book they are writing. They re-read what they've written and want to throw it away. They should throw away their perfectionism and buy a plastic bag instead. Fill it first and re-read after!

It wrecks people's holidays. They expect perfection from a cheap package and sulk when heaven isn't included with the hotel.

Perfection wrecks relationships too. People try so hard to find their perfect partner who doesn't exist, they don't see the possibilities in their real partners who do.

But Hebrew hasn't got 'perfect', it's got the word Tam, which doesn't mean making no mistakes or being someone you aren't or can't be. It means complete, whole and wholesome.

On my father's tombstone in the cemetery I read the text 'Mark the perfect man'. Now Pa never pretended to be perfect. He had a temper and he knew it, but he used it to defend defenceless stray dogs and down and outs. Being big-hearted he could make mistakes. He once brought two mangy, flea-ridden stray dogs to my mother, as she was attempting her first dinner party. Pa proceeded to bathe them and anoint them before the startled diners! 'They would want to see them aired,' he asserted. Ma, who hardly drinks, swallowed two stiff brandies.

Pa was no pale shadow of perfection, he was a humane human being with no snobbery or pretence. The prim English translation on his tomb didn't do him justice. The homelier Hebrew did.

# To the bones below St Peter's

I was relieved when Canon Colin Semper said he never used to like Westminster Abbey, because I've never liked St Peter's in Rome either. I just can't pray in it. There's too much marble, too many tourists clicking cameras, too many wriggling saints. The fountains in front are nice but they need green English grass not gravel or stone around them.

But on my last visit, I saw St Peter's from below, which is better. Here's how you do it. Face the church and walk round it on the left. When you're challenged by the Swiss Guards, say you want the Office for Excavations. In the office show your passport, fill out a form, and look sober and serious, then they'll telephone your hotel later to tell you you can go below with a priest in tow.

Below the church you're in an ancient Roman city of the dead. You file through narrow alleys, and peer into the tombs of people who passed away 2,000 years ago. I felt embarrassed because it seemed like prying.

Then we stopped in front of a wall. We're now below the main altar – we all wanted to know one thing – is St Peter present or not?

Well, beneath the main altar is a medieval one, and beneath that a late Roman one, and below that is a 'trophy', a memorial, but there aren't any bones in it. They've gone – perhaps they were scattered when Rome was raided. No one knows.

But there is a wall with Christian scratchmarks and these point to a place in it and there they found human remains – I saw them myself through a hole. The scientists say they're those of a strong, stocky man, past middle life, who lived in the first century.

I don't know what you think but perhaps they're Peter's and it isn't because of all that pomp on top, which to be honest turns me off.

There's a bar in St Peter's complete with coffee machine and cocktails. It's hidden away, and needs hunting out. But it's a good place to sit back and consider that the great building you are leaning against rests on such small and perplexing remains.

But then all organised religion, with its bank accounts and committees and office blocks and computers rests on equally slender things. Jacob's dream about a ladder, dead bones linking together in Ezekiel's imagination and the experience of the disciples of the presence of Jesus, after he died. I know from my own experience how strong the slender things of

77

religion are. Many years ago I started chattering to an unseen something. I felt silly talking to someone who wasn't there but I staked my life and my livelihood on It, and It was powerful enough to transform me and underpin me as securely as St Peter's in Rome.

# *Journey Through a Religious Year*

If you follow the Jewish liturgy and its cycle of festivals, you'll accompany the children of Israel as they flee from Egypt, wander through the desert, meet God at Sinai, and come to the borders of a Promised Land. En route you will acquire a working knowledge of sin, transgression, temptation and atonement.

If you follow the Christian liturgy you'll accompany Christ through his birth, baptism, passion and resurrection. You will journey together from Galilee to Jerusalem. Hopefully new life will also blossom in you en route.

Both are uncomfortable journeys, so they have been sentimentalised with robins, reindeer, conspicuous consumption and role playing.

They are now covered in so much tat, it is a struggle to unwrap their real message and relate it to your own life. These are my attempts to break through the packaging. I hope they help you.

# Grising trains (Passover)

The train which takes me three hours on weekdays, takes me five on Sundays. I've no complaints. I like long train journeys, peering into people's back-gardens, examining their roofs, their smalls on the clothes line, and the gnomes that screen their dust-bins.

I was first attracted to trains during the evacuation. I had seen my first Hitchcock film, and the dreary, draughty wartime carriages became glamorous with sultry spies and Mata Haris with lots of lovers and dead bodies.

Some of the romance has faded of course. Steam has been replaced by diesel, my favourite fruit pies by enormous buns in plastic bags, and the tchka, tchka, tchka of personal cassette players drives everyone crazy, but not with love. But a railway carriage is still the best place to write a sermon, because the realities of life and religion become very clear in crowded trains.

I need this realism for I'm a religious professional, so concerned with rituals I sometimes forget what they represent. You may have the same problems as you

81

make the elaborate preparations required for the great religious festivals such as Passover, Easter or the devotions of Holy Week.

Take matzos for example – the unleavened Passover bread. It's not enough to eat them and call them 'the bread of the poor' in ancient Aramaic. I realised this in a crowded second class carriage where there was no buffet for the poor passengers who were standing while the first class dining coaches were empty. It wasn't right and the matzo reminded me I ought to do something about it – though to be honest I don't know what.

And Easter means more than chanting gospel passages about the resurrection. It means rising up yourself and giving up your seat when it's needed, though you've reserved it.

Station queues and crowded compartments are true tests of our compassion and integrity, for then we are compressed into one body willy nilly, not in faith but in fact.

Last year I also learnt an important lesson when my Sunday train stopped at a deserted station. I wandered out and chatted to a griser taking down train numbers with frozen fingers. 'What are you going to do with those numbers, mate?' I asked facetiously. 'Add them up?' No he wasn't going to tell them to friends, nor enter them for competitions. He spotted trains because he loved them, that's all. I've thought about him a lot since, hoping my love of God might one day be as pure.

# The rise and fall of Smith (Easter Monday)

My Christian colleagues take services on Sundays, and when I do *Thought for the Day* on Mondays I hope they can have a lie in. I wasn't sure if they would want me on Easter Monday though, because I think it's the most critical day of the Christian year. Now I'm not ignorant, I know most churches are closed on that day, but it's still critical, and I'll use my Mr Smith to explain why. Now you can't know him, because I've just invented him. But you'll recognise him, because there's a bit of you in him and a lot of me.

He's an ordinary guy, who was inoculated against real religion in Sunday school. But one year, because of some rumblings in his stomach or on the stock-market, he felt insecure and decided on impulse to give up nut chocolate for Lent. His self-denial might also help him wriggle into his holiday pants when he goes to Tenerife.

The Church service dismayed him though. There were two or three pounds of prayers to get through. But the music brought back his childhood and this made him feel sentimental, then saintly. Under its influence he put more in the collection-plate than he intended and scarcely regretted it. The Easter service brought tears to his eyes and he decided to turn over a new leaf. Perhaps he'd take Mrs Smith to Tenerife too.

He left Church in a gentle mood, which so startled Mrs Smith that she dropped a sauce boat, and became speechless when Smithie picked up the pieces and gave her a glass of his precious port. They had a lovely Easter dinner with wine and felt like a family again.

But the wine gave Mr Smith a hangover and next morning he had words with Mrs Smith about the bacon. Now she's upset and takes it out on Master Smith, who takes it out on their dog, Fluffy.

Mr Smith invokes heaven to testify to his innocence, stamps out, and blasphemes when he arrives at the pub too early. It's his first relapse into sin since his religious rebirth and Easter Monday marks his fall. Over his bitter he decides to chuck religion as it changes nothing.

Now I'd like to give him and you some advice. Be patient! It takes time for grace to do its work in you – a lifetime. And it's harder being fair to your family than to strangers, because there's more expectation. Liturgy, you see, deals in blacks and whites, but in daily life you have to distinguish between different shades of grey, which is much more difficult. So pick yourself up and don't give up when things go wrong. I know there's no religious mood-music to help you on dead days, like Easter Monday, but there may be unexpected sermons (if you're not too snobbish to spot them). 'Love is a many splendoured thing', whether it's preached from a pulpit or someone sings it from a juke box.

And one last tip. After any religious service, give the

door a good look as you go out, and ask yourself how you're going to get your religion through it. If you can't, is it more real than *Dallas* or *Dynasty*? That's what makes Easter Monday so critical. Take care now!

# *Two presents for the New Year*

Before the sun sets and the Jewish New Year begins, people give presents to each other and to the poor, and greetings which take the form of food. They serve slices of honey cake and apple dipped in honey, so that the coming year may be sweet for all.

I can't give you a taste of honey cake through a printed page, but I can make you a present of two stories, one serious, the other silly. The serious one took a load off me last year and I hope it will help you too. I've heard it told about holy rabbis, monks and gurus. So take your pick.

A holy man was on a pilgrimage with his young disciple. They journeyed on till they came to a swollen river. A young beautiful girl was sobbing beside the bank, because she couldn't swim across.

Straightaway the old man signed to her to climb on his back. Clinging to him, her young flesh pressing on his, and her arms clasped round his chest, he carried her across the river. At the other side he let her down. Shyly she kissed him and went her way. The young disciple couldn't keep his disapproval to himself. 'Master!' he burst out. The older man turned, but the younger one could not continue, and the two trudged on in silence.

Eating their frugal meal that night, the young man could not contain himself. 'Master,' he said again, 'you saw how young and beautiful she was! How could you risk your inner peace and let her come so close to you, her flesh clinging to yours, as you carried her across the river?'

The old man looked up at his disciple in surprise. 'What,' he said in astonishment, 'do you still carry her?'

Now you and I have done some pretty dreadful things in our past but you don't have to carry them into your future. It's simple enough to unload them. If you've hurt someone, do them a good turn instead. If that's not possible, do it to someone else. Say sorry to God if you believe in Him, and to yourself if you don't. Then put it down to experience and call it a day and remind yourself that tomorrow is the beginning of the rest of your life. If you can't forgive yourself, you'll never be able to forgive anybody else.

Well, that's my present to you and if you prefer honey cake I'm sorry, but you can't please everybody all the time.

Now here's my second present.

There was this man who was paying for a kosher cookbook at the cash desk.

'Do you cook?' asked the salesgirl.

'No, it's a New Year present for my wife.'

'What a practical present,' she said, 'you'll give her a lovely surprise.'

'Won't I just,' he answered, 'she was expecting dinner at the Dorch.'

# The art of suffering (Day of Atonement)

When the ram's horn sounds, and three stars appear (or ought to) in the sky, the Jewish Day of Atonement begins, and I recite a lot of prayers. Most I go along with but one or two bits I leave out and hope no one notices. It's no use telling God what He knows I can't say sincerely.

I have always had trouble with this sentence, 'Thou O God art just in all that has come upon us, for Thou hast done justly, but we have acted wickedly.' For me it's over the top. A lot of the suffering in my life is my own fault, but at my Last Judgment God has also got some explaining to do.

Before I became a rabbi, I used to worry why people suffered. I bought books about it by Jewish mystics, Christians, and Buddhists. But after I qualified, I no longer had time to read them. I had to make too many visits, and when I got home I read Georgette Heyer instead, just to relax.

But I learnt a lot on those visits on how to suffer and I

pass it on to you. You can't cure suffering but you aren't helpless either.

Don't despise small things. A cup of sweet tea helps after a shock, and a mug of it even more. If you wake up with nightmares, keep a happy book by your bed. You could try a cook book, because each recipe has an inbuilt happy ending. Holy objects, prayer books, rosaries and religious medals help in pain. They're something solid to clutch on to.

Get your suffering outside you. Turn it into a letter or short story, or draw it on a piece of paper. If you're not up to creative stuff, complain to a friend. If your problem is you've got no friend, ring the Samaritans, or capture a young clergyman, who has to listen, but you needn't take his advice.

If you've been ditched, but still got stamina, ask the young clergyman if he's got a singles club going at his church. If he hasn't play on his guilt and get one going.

If you're worried about being ditched by another single, try God. I did and it's my great lasting relationship. Thirty-eight years and still going strong.

Don't get snobbish about your suffering. It isn't a punishment for your sins, nor a reward for your virtue. It's part of being human – that's the name of the game. I thought I had a foretaste of hell after some dreadful dreams. But it was only the side effects of some tablets. The specialist reduced the dose, which halted my private horror show.

Because you're human, allow yourself to scream or moan, or buy a salt beef sandwich, or a second opinion. God prefers humility to heroics.

And talking of God . . .

'Ah,' I know you're thinking, 'he had to get the God bit in didn't he, because that's the name of his game . . .'

Well, why not? It's a practical though puzzling bit. If you offer your suffering to God, it seems to turn it inside out and gives your pain some meaning. Though what it means I'm not sure. Are you?

It's a hard life being human, my grandpa said, but it's interesting and you don't die of boredom.

# Christmas in Majorca

I was at the end of my tether after a hectic year. I'd ended up as a male agony aunt on TV who could be wise about everybody else's problems except my own. So I asked a friend in the travel trade to package me. She took one look at me and promptly put me on a plane to Palma, Majorca.

The hotel was comfy and worked hard to make us happy. Flamenco dancers snorted and stamped in front of me, and I tried to cry out Arriba with the rest. I voted for our hotel's very own wonderwoman on an electric clapometer and stood in line to get my false nose from Santa.

But while waiting, I went under, drowning in despair as I remembered friendships that had failed, and my own mistakes repeated many times.

Lots of people feel that way around Christmas time,

for forced fun is worse than none, and the loneliest place is in a crowd.

Next day, I escaped in a hired car and drove to a hermitage high in the hills above Palma. It was still and silent, and the hermits stayed hidden which was only right and proper.

On the parapet in the rays of the setting sun, I turned my mind to the afterlife because I'd made such a mess of this one. But did I believe in it? I'm not good at believing and how could I? For when I die, time and space will die with me, so there won't be any 'after'.

But luckily I don't have to believe in eternal life, because I've experienced it. Sitting in silent synagogues and churches I had touched it. And it had touched me too, quite roughly, turfing me out of my seat on crowded trains, and making me give up more than I intended.

High up in the hermitage I sat in silence and eternity touched me again. For the first time in months I stopped worrying.

Reluctantly I returned to my hotel. The flamenco dancers must have collapsed with fatigue because the bar was now full of Majorcan bagpipers. I wanted to sneak away but you can't be a spoilsport after a spiritual experience. So I munched a mince pie, put on a paper hat and asked another single to dance. It was that dreadful chicken dance, and we chirped, wriggled, and waggled our way into the New Year. To my surprise I enjoyed it.

And this was very nice for me, but what is in it for you?

Two things. First discover eternal life for yourself. Fifteen minutes of silence in any holy place, repeated several times will do it. Don't discuss it, get on with it. It's waiting for you.

Secondly, eternity isn't far in the future. It's that part of the present which makes it worthwhile. It's tucked into it, like a hole in a mint, or a cherry in a chocolate. When you've discovered it, you won't have to be sad in a super hotel suite. You can even be happy in a hermitage.

# Concerning Christmas – a rabbi's tips

The real reason I became a rabbi was to spite my parents. At least that's what I overheard my mother telling my father, and she's a shrewd cookie. 'I don't care whether he thinks he's Jeremiah or Joan of Arc – mark my words, Harry – he's doing it to spite us.' Of course I maintained it was the holy spirit. But a wicked grin kept curling my lips, and I couldn't keep it back.

My new holiness certainly made life hot for them. My mother had to reorganise her kitchen, and they both had to eat their forbidden food in the loo. But that was their problem, and I washed my hands of them. I couldn't make a mess of my salvation just to keep them happy.

In any case, if I was frank with myself, which I wasn't, I didn't quite want them to be too happy. Though I loved them, there were some old scores to pay off. They were so anxious to get me out of the ghetto, they had fixed my career while I was in my cot, and I was too small to carry all their expectation. 'You'll be a solicitor,' they moaned at me, 'a solicitor, a solicitor, a sh'missiter.' They meant it for my own good, but they could have given Comrade Mao lessons in brainwashing babies. They saved to send me to college, and did without to buy me books. They were

so self-sacrificing I couldn't cope, and opted for a career in religion because it muddled them.

I can admit all this now because it doesn't matter. Somewhere along the way I fell in love with love and found faith, and as they got older my parents liked to have an expert on heaven around, because it was coming appreciably nearer.

Now this snippet of autobiography has a message for you as any festival approaches, when you are being got at, from the press, the pulpit and the idiot box. It is a simple message – don't carry too much expectation with you or expect your friends or family to carry it for you.

First a tip about food. You don't have to force feed your guests, to appease your inferiority complex. If you prefer fish fingers to turkey, at Christmas for example, why not? After all, the apostles ate fish, but never tasted turkey. They're nice (the fish fingers I mean, not the apostles), fried with garlic and anchovy sauce.

And that brings me to drinks. If you can't afford to put on the style, serve honest ale or lemonade but don't economise with 'cup' or punch. How can people judge their capacity if you've mixed a tin of peaches into a bottle of plonk?

And don't make your family miserable by forcing them to be merry. Why force them to play happy families? They're entitled to their moods, and to be religious you must first of all be real.

# *Travel Broadens The Mind*

In the middle ages, students wandered from university to university to find their special teacher, and when they found him, they followed him across frontiers to learn from him.

My formal education rejected all this as romantic. I was cajoled to pass an exam (like the clever monkey I was). Then I was sent to do a diploma or degree course at any college which would give me a grant. The object was a piece of paper, which some graduates framed and hung over their desks.

My real education was quite different, and I received it on the hoof, through listening to people and watching them as they revealed the tangles of their lives. And in their muddles, I sometimes spotted a glittering thread of eternal life knotted among the other threads of work, sex, family and self-interest.

My spiritual education therefore took place in doughnut parlours, bus queues, hippy communes, and bars. Some were respectable, many were not. God was present in all of them.

I couldn't learn much about God on home ground. I had to travel to find him. Why? I am not sure. I think at home, I was too protected and defended. A house is like a castle, and nothing new could break through to me.

# Hip, hip, hippie!

The telephone rang. It was from Amsterdam. Could I come over, and give a Sunday sermon at Paradiso? I blinked, for Paradiso was the haunt of the Amsterdam hippies in my student days. Why a sermon from me – now I was rotted by success and rather establishment? I agreed straightaway, though I was far too busy. But I owed a lot to the hippies – they took me in once, when I was really down and nobody wanted to know.

People are too insecure to have much time for hippies now. When people's prosperity is threatened, their tolerance dries up with their money. And hippies could certainly be trying. I giggled myself when droopy girls pressed dying daisies into my hand outside the Hilton, and I never understood why they were for beards and against bras. More seriously some of them were degraded by the drugs they dabbled in so trustingly. And the hard-headed world they rejected, highjacked them. It turned them into a high-fashion industry and made money out of them.

The hippy commune that took me in didn't use money. They lived off food that was free. So we ate mushrooms, served in many ways, grilled, stewed or psychedelic. But I got apprehensive when one guest saw visions after supper. 'What types of mushrooms do you eat?' I asked nervously. 'Every type Mother Nature provides,' they said, 'but some we eat only once.' I went out and bought my own baked beans. They also taught me to cook rice. We contemplated it, and then burnt it.

They were better with religion than rice. They believed in original goodness, not original sin, and this belief made them very caring. They nursed a sick Chinese sailor until he died, sleeping beside him in bed, holding him close to comfort him because he felt so alone. They also taught a poor persecuted Turk to trust again. And three amorous Americans introduced me to a commune of transvestites, who were not figures of fun. At four in the morning they found places on the floor for people whom the police and professionals couldn't bother or cope with. I'm not up to that sort of love and I've lost the innocence of the hippies, if I ever had it, but they taught me to accept people as they are, and not as I wanted them to be, and to listen to people's lives before I used them for moral lessons.

So when I'm back in Amsterdam, I might look them up, though it was over thirty years ago. 'Why here's Lionel,' they'll say. 'Find the old B a blanket and grill him some mushrooms.' And I'll say hurriedly and hypocritically, 'No, no, please don't trouble yourself, I'll buy my own baked beans.'

# The Golden Country

There were two of us who wanted to train for the Reform Jewish ministry after the war but where were we going to do it? For our last seminary was closed in Berlin in 1941. The obvious course was to send us to study in America and I liked the idea because I fancied myself in a charcoal grey suit, thinking clean thoughts and saying, 'Yes Ma'am'. But the powers that be preferred to reassemble the remnants of old Berlin and set up a seminary for two in Golders Green, London, England. Officially, because they were concerned for Jewish survival in Europe, unofficially because they were worried we wouldn't come back.

And they had reason, because for the poor, persecuted Jews of Eastern Europe, from whom I am descended, although the Promised Land lay in the Middle East, the land of promise lay in quite a different direction, way out west. They called it in Yiddish the Golden Medina, the Golden Country, and went through fire and water to get there.

I finally made it to America years later on a lecture tour and I loved the exuberance of Jewish life over there. In New York, Chinese restaurants' fortune cookies broke open to reveal texts from the Talmud and the synagogues were dreamy. Electronic pulpits rose in the air, holy arks were self-opening and the spot lights got a blue rinse whenever the bereaved recalled their dear departed. Of course I wrote letters home deploring such shenanigans but secretly I longed to minister in such places.

Well, I had my chance and I muffed it. I was taken to a meeting of young middle class couples, who were setting up a new synagogue in a suburb. They were a generous lot who wanted the best rabbi their resources could procure. The salary they decided on seemed stupendous to me and would mean many sacrifices for them. They considered quite reasonably that the fortunate rabbi so chosen would have to be successful and produce results. To spur him on and keep him on his toes he would only be given a short contract. I nearly got that job, but I dithered and didn't. Firstly, because I'm still not sure what religious results are. All you can do is convert yourself and the rest is a gift of God. Secondly, a religious person must be able to stand aside from success and at such a salary I couldn't afford to be a failure. But God often wants to work through failures! Sometimes that's just what he wants us to be. And if that's how he wants us, then accepting failure as a friend is a necessity for a religious person.

So I said goodbye to the Golden Country, and came back to queue for my fish and chips with other failures in NW6, London, England, where Hampstead collapses into Kilburn.

# Poor fish

I came back from Germany where they wanted to know why I believed in God. They meant business because they booked a big hall, as they thought other people might like to know too.

And this showed great courage on their part, because the more heavy and serious they got, the more nervous I became, and horrible things happened.

They sat me high up on a podium with a mike, a sheaf of paper, and in case one of my precious words was wasted, a stenographer to take notes in German shorthand.

I peered over the podium and dropped a pencil on a professor which made him angry, and me twitchy. So I spilt the water, and it trickled over the stenographer, who grabbed the mike to move it away from me. I knew I was a disaster area, so I chewed on a pencil, but got the wrong end and swallowed the point.

'Er is dumm,' (he's a fool) – I heard one serious lady sigh in German to another. 'Well-meaning but a fool!'

'Why do you come?' I heard the other ask curiously. 'For the recipes,' said the first. 'I hear he has a way with fish.'

I gaze at her with astonishment, and quickly launch into my lecture to prevent any more personal remarks.

I lead them a merry chase up medieval philosophy, and how it proves God does exist and a less merry chase down modern philosophy and how it proves He doesn't. They cover page after page with notes they will never read again.

I get to the end, and pause, and know I can't leave it like that. 'Please put away your notes,' I say firmly, 'and listen to me.' I fall down from the podium, pick myself up, and sit among them. 'Perhaps he will give us a fish recipe now,' whispers the lady.

I look at her, smile, and commence. 'We human beings are pretty poor fish really.' She starts to write, then looks uncertain and stops. 'We like people who like us, and are generous when we've got more than enough for ourselves. Such love is nice, human and natural. But in my life I've met a few people, whose love has been more than natural, supernatural if you like, super–duper–natural and they are the real reason why I believe.'

One of them was a German woman I knew. After the war she had hardly any food but she sent whatever she had to the German refugees, fleeing from the Poles in the east. Now that was nice but natural because everybody loves their own. But then she prayed and began to spend parcels to the poor Poles, who were occupying the homes of those same German refugees. 'It isn't natural,' said her neighbours. And it wasn't! It was silly and supernatural, that's all.

The real reason I believe in God, is not because anybody's proved Him, but because I've met Him – in her, for example.

I finish the lecture. It leaves some puzzled and some relieved. I had gone on longer than I expected, and I had only a few minutes to get my bus. The serious lady surges up to me, 'Rabbiner Blue, Rabbiner Blue, I want a Jewish fish recipe.' I've no time and start to tell her so. Then I remember my friend who had food for everybody. 'Sit down,' I say. I give her a recipe of my grandmother's, who fed a whole street of families in the slump.

I miss my bus, but that's the price you pay. As I walk home I realise I haven't just given my lecture, I've begun to live it. In the dark I bump into someone, say sorry, and find it's only a tree. I feel foolish but very happy.

If you want to find out if God is alive for you, lectures can be helpful, but you also have to help yourself. So do something silly, supernatural, and generous for God's sake. That's how faith comes. It's foolish but it's fun.

# FKK in Yugoslavia

It was the first day of my holiday in Yugoslavia, and I was trying to find the bathing beach. There was a sign but it didn't say 'bathing' or 'beach', just 'FKK'. Now what did that mean I wondered, but there were no other signs, so I trudged up the straight and narrow path it pointed to. At the end was another sign, which looked like a road sign but wasn't, because on a motorway it would have caused a multiple crash. It showed a black pair of pants or bloomers, ringed in a red circle, and overpainted with a black cross. I had strayed on to a naturist beach, which are everywhere in Yugoslavia.

I marched fearlessly on to the rocks, and promptly tripped up over two elderly ladies in starkers, who were chewing salami while they laid out their picnic. They were tourists from the Fatherland, and we chortled together for two or three minutes in basic Teutonic. They must have thought me shifty, because I couldn't look them in the eye – or indeed anywhere else. They proudly showed me pictures of their nice, naked grandchildren.

Then they pointed to my toes, and jabbered a lot and wagged their heads and hands. There were prickly plants in the water and I must wear plastic sandals when I went in. I didn't have any. Never mind, said my grannies, I could wear theirs.

And that is how I came to be poised over the bright blue water, clad in plastic high heels and not much else. That's my story and I'm sticking to it.

But then a boat of sightseers sailed by. Well, I was the sight they saw, and it must have given them something to think about, because they brought out binoculars which unnerved me. I tried to creep behind a rock, but disturbed a lizard, which made me jump, and I belly flopped into the water, kicking up my high heels as I shot in. Those sightseers certainly had their money's worth.

When they went away, I crawled out from the water, very nude and nervous and sat in the sun, thinking over the theology of bodies.

There's certainly a lot of confusion in it. Although this incident for example may sound orgiastic it was nothing of the sort. For naked bodies are very matter of fact. Lust doesn't live in our bodies, but in our minds and our imagination. You get less sexual stimulus from looking at ageing, burnt flesh on a beach than you do from staring at high class dummies in high street windows. Clothes, I thought, don't cover attraction, they create it. Perhaps that's why fashion is so popular.

And after all the same God who created my mind and soul also fashioned my body, and according to tradition, it is not refuse, but will one day share in their resurrection. I remembered too how I had once jumped into the road to push away a child who nearly got caught under a car. There was no time for my mind to think, but my body instinctively jumped forward to save the kid.

According to the Bible, God gave us bowels of compassion. Well, it's our duty to exercise them in His service. So use your arms to cuddle someone who needs support, and your lips for a kiss of forgiveness to heal a hurt. A hug will show your kindness and compassion more than any words.

As I left the beach, my grannies were knitting away, with upright needles in the continental manner and chewing chocolate. They waved for me to sit beside them, but I declined politely, for parts of me I hadn't expected were turning too pink and painful to sit on. Which was a pity as I wanted to ask them what FKK stood for. Any guesses?

# Hitching to Heaven

In hospital they put a long thin thing up my groin and into my heart, and watched what happened on a screen. They made it so pleasant, even I became curious and said I'd watch it too. It looked like a worm crawling about in a cod cutlet.

I was relieved when they trundled me back on my trolley, because I've always liked movement and free rides, and the memories of my hitchhiking days made me forget the cod cutlet.

When school ended, I used to stagger to the continent with my rucksack and hitchhike on the road out of Calais. If my first lift turned left, I spent the summer in Scandinavia with blondes on beaches. If it turned right, I headed for Rome, expressos and religion.

I ganged up with a girl who used me and a pepper pot to protect her honour. While she showed a leg and hitched, I hid behind a hedge and drank watered wine.

When something stopped I rushed out with our rucksacks grubby with wine stains and grinning invitingly. But our lifts took one look at this apparition and shot off, leaving me flat on my back. I don't blame them, because though I sported a Union Jack, I looked more like Jack the Ripper than a representative of clean cut English youth.

But some did stop, for people are surprisingly kind.

I remember a worker priest on a tiny scooter took us both aboard. But my rucksack overbalanced him and we all fell in a heap into the municipal flowerbed in Aix en Provence, and were shooed out of town. A former SS officer gave us a lift. So did a confidence trickster, who cheated us out of our few francs.

In the fifties the highways were festooned with hitchhikers like me – most of them more presentable and polite. So I had a lot of time to meditate, hidden in my hedgerows. While waiting I mulled over a tattered book I'd bought in a Youth Hostel for fifteen old francs – it was a children's version of Bunyan's *Pilgrim's Progress* in French.

And it changed my attitude to hitchhiking. I began to realise that the miles didn't matter. It wasn't important how many kilometres of dusty road we covered, for whatever the road signs said, we were also on quite another journey and eternity was our destination.

This knowledge helped me not to hate the drivers who sped by in smart cars honking at poor hitch-hikers. It helped me too when my girl friend decided to go it alone because she could make better speed without me.

When you know you are also travelling to God, you don't feel so forlorn or lonely. And as they trundled me back on my trolley down hospital corridors, I imagined I was hitching again as in the old days. I had after all ridden on even odder lifts – a hearse for example. But the destination hadn't changed. I was still on my way to heaven.

# Serious Travel or 'My Son, the Conference Delegate!'

I used to like organising conferences, because I fancied myself as a 'fixer'. I had low tastes. I liked being in the inner circle, in the know, among those who mattered, lording it over the suckers, who sat in the back rows.

It was quite deplorable, and unspeakably vulgar, and I am thankful I grew out of it before I corrupted myself completely. As I became more secure, I didn't need such false reassurance.

I still go to conferences sometimes as a speaker. But as soon as I decently can, I retire to the back rows I once despised. There I suck sweets, chew gum, and exchange ribald remarks with other delegates and observers. It's much more fun.

Wisdom rarely comes from a key note address or

from any platform exhortation – they are too ponder-ous. It surfaces in corridors, over cups of tea, and at the conference bar. Now I no longer want to manage people, I enjoy them instead!

# My big behind in the back row

I was attending a conference of caring people. I sat bored stiff in the back row, peering into my neighbour's notes. He wasn't listening either, but totting up some figures. Carefully he crossed out a fourteen and substituted a thirteen. 'What's that?' I whispered. 'It's my calorie count,' he replied hoarsely. 'How many calories in that new slimming sweet – made of seaweed and saccharine?' I passed his question along the back row, and a heated discussion about diets took place in the canteen afterwards.

Munching cream cakes, comfort eaters all, we recited our confessions of faith. Some believed in calories and some in carbohydrates.

Two social workers swore by bananas and cream. You could have as much as you liked of either, but nothing else. Well the first day was fine. They guzzled a big bowl for breakfast, and for supper two more. But breakfast next day didn't seem so nice, and at supper they snarled at each other.

On day three, they broke, and they rushed to the

butcher, bought two pounds of steak, and a bottle of wine to wash it down. The neighbours heard them singing 'Yes We Have No Bananas' before they went to bed. It was rather embarrassing.

A rabbi confessed to nightly noshes. He had fixed a lock to his fridge, and told his wife to hide the key. 'Did it work?' No, he kept a secret reserve of smoked salmon in his study.

A vicar added that the only diet which worked with him was the Seafood Diet. We looked up hopefully – how much was allowed? He gave a grim laugh, 'I see food, then I eat it'.

When they went, I consumed the last cake, wondering why all our diets went wrong. In times of stress, a big black hole opened up inside us, but however much food we shovelled into it, we never felt full.

Then I realised what was wrong. What we hungered for wasn't food at all, but affection. We who cared for others, couldn't comfort ourselves.

So here's my advice, if you find yourself rummaging through the larder for a large bag of biscuits – don't! Biscuits won't work. Stop feeling a failure and try to like yourself instead.

Here are two sayings of the rabbis to help you. The first from a lovely man called Rabbi Zusya – 'In the coming world,' he said, 'they won't ask why I wasn't Moses, but only why I wasn't Zusya.' So don't apologise for not being Mother Teresa or Albert Schweitzer, or your own grandpa. God wants you to be you. You're unique, a one off, that's how he made you.

The second saying is practical. 'At the Last Judgment God will ask you "Why didn't you enjoy all the nice things I permitted you?"' Well what sort of things? Why not drape that multi-coloured towel round your middle and rhumba round the room? Bright clothes brighten your feelings. Or lie on your back and wave your feet in the air, if that's how you feel. Because it's fun, it isn't sinful or foolish. And you can sing this hymn, my colleague the very reverend Rabbi Dr Jonathan Magonet wrote in his student days, before he became quite so reverend. It's called 'The Belly Bossanova'.

The Belly Bossanova is so easy to do.
It's a Latin variation of the old one two.
You wiggle your belly and your big behind
And you take a lot of weight off your mind.

He was right. It isn't our bellies that need nourishment. It's our minds and souls that are starved. That's why we feel so hungry.

# By the waters of Lake Geneva

By the waters of Lake Geneva, I sat down and ate. I would have wept if I had had to pay the bill, which I didn't because a generous clergyman was going to pay it for me. I liked him a lot for he was caring as well as competent. I used to watch him at high-powered committee meetings. When he closed his eyes, I turned off too, because he knew, two hours of tedium in advance, where we would all arrive at.

But as he tucked into a bowl of white asparagus with melted butter, I knew all was not well and that his spirit groaned within him. 'They want to make me a bishop,' he said moodily. 'About time too. You'll make a jolly good one – and enjoy it. Let's drink to it.'

'That's the trouble Lionel,' he said sadly, filling his glass and mine with Lacrima Christi, a Swiss wine more secular than it sounds, 'I'll enjoy it too much, which is worldly and a sin.' He shook his head and finished the bottle.

'Does success work that way?' I wondered. A little worldly success usually makes me a lot nicer. But most of us never get enough of the stuff to find out.

While he ordered another bottle, I looked thoughtfully at the other diners, beautiful people who toyed with tiny soufflés in puddles of expensive raspberry juice. The subtle notes of their aftershave blended with the blackberry nose of their wine. What was God's word to them?

'God doesn't only love the poor,' I said slowly, 'that's just our envy and sentimentalism. His love is universal – so it includes successful clerics like you, and middle class people like me, and yuppies, gumpies and dinkies, living in LAT relationships.' 'What's a LAT relationship?' he asked, interested in spite of himself. 'Living apart but together.'

'So you think it's my duty to accept?' he asked hopefully. 'Well in religion it's simpler, spiritually speaking, if you're at the top or the bottom of the

114

sandwich – a holy bishop or holy beggar. It's more complicated when you're the filling in the middle like me.'

'But do be careful, dear,' I said, leaning over the table impulsively. 'Don't get addicted to success. It's easy come and easy go, and when it goes, don't let your niceness go with it. Enjoy it, but don't depend on it.'

This conversation took place many years ago, but I always add the same caution whenever I wish people worldly secular success. It's good stuff if you can get it, and know how to use it.

And you needn't feel guilty about it, because it's so easy to make it sacred and hallow it. All you have to do is pass your happiness on to others. You could for example invite some deserving clergyman like me to a slap-up meal he couldn't otherwise afford. God's word to the successful is simple – don't keep it to yourself! Spread it around, spread it around – that's all!


# *A present from Berlin*

I was chatting at a conference with a nice clergyman and my friend Dr Wendy Greengross who specialises in problems which are special but real, such as sex for handicapped people. We were wondering whether it was ethical to recycle presents. After all what can you do with a dozen packs of bath salts when you only have time for showers?

Then I told them about a letter from an old lady who only had her pension. Could I make any suggestions for presents even poor people like her could give?

Well we put our heads together and here are some we thought up and they're suitable for rich people too, because the pressies which matter most are those in which people give their imagination and time as well as their belongings.

If someone's lonely, a telephone call is a low cost present. Ten pence makes all the difference between feeling loved or left out.

You can also give someone something which is truly priceless, like giving up a grudge against him or her.

But when giving presents remember two 'auld acquaintances' people forget whatever lists they make. First what about a present to yourself?

Give yourself some free time. It's no good trying to do too much, and crying into your cranberry sauce. Take some time to walk in the park or a quiet street, and not be a perfect parent, or a happy hostess for a while, just yourself.

Give yourself permission to do something you normally don't allow yourself. A whole day in bed can be depressing, but a late morning lie-in is lovely with a cup of tea and a transistor.

The most useful pressie I received last year was a recipe someone had written out for me. I've never been good at cakes, and this is the only one that doesn't become a biscuit. She also told me to mix a bottle of mincemeat into my cake mixture and get a short cut Christmas cake.

If you're handy about the house, help someone who

isn't, to fix a leaky tap, or a fuse. If you're helpless like me, it's worth more than barrels of bath salts.

You can also do something for somebody, you don't like doing for yourself, like cleaning a cooker – provided you know what you're doing and can put it back together.

What about putting away your ordinary cheque book and writing out a cheque on your time. 'I promise to give my friend two hours of my time on demand to use in whatever way my friend wishes, provided it's not illegal, immoral or fattening.'

There are also pressies you can give, which cost hardly any money, like a cup of tea in a kitchen and a long listen. It's worth all the loot of Bond Street.

What about giving yourself back your past – the nice parts of it that is. Go and see an old friend you've often thought of, but haven't set eyes on for years. Have a 'do you remember?' session together.

The other present people forget is the one for God. I think the only thing you can give Him directly is your attention. So sit in a place where people worship, when there's no official service going on, and give Him ten minutes of time.

The prophet Isaiah called out to all who were thirsty and hungry. You can have food and drink, he said, without a bill or price ticket. I often wondered what on earth he meant. Now I know. There's a lot of nourishment in the milk of human kindness. And what does it cost you?

# *Put me down gently*

I was invited to a retreat for alcoholics and I accepted because they don't play religious games, but take their spirituality neat, like the spirits they no longer drink. We chatted about put downs, those daily deadly pin-pricks which could send them racing back to the bottle, and me to the fridge in a frenzy of comfort eating.

I suffered from put downs most when I was an adolescent. I remember ringing up a girl to date her. Through some fault of the switchboard, though I could hear her, she couldn't hear me. She was giggling about me to another girl and I felt like a scalded cat. I never saw her again – which was a pity because I found out later she fancied me.

A former actor at the retreat said you could learn a lot from theatre people about putting up with put downs. He used to know Eric Maschkowitz who was responsible for the big hit *Good Night Vienna*. Well one evening Eric stopped at some traffic lights in Lewisham, and saw *Good Night Vienna* was playing at the local Empire. He went in incognito and casually asked the manager how it was doing. 'Hmm,' the manager pondered, 'as well as *Good Night Lewisham* would do in Vienna.'

The same thing happened to me a few weeks ago in the synagogue when an old lady came up to me after the service. 'Rabbi,' she said, 'you sounded so sincere this week.' 'Thank you,' I replied meekly.

And I pass on this lesson I've learnt from theatre people and politicians – don't take put downs too heavily or hide them. Tell them out aloud and turn your torment into a joke. That's how you become a comic. The only put downs to take seriously are those which come from heaven not human beings.

Last year, I lay awake during my first night in hospital, wondering if I would ever get out. I had helped many people make their peace with death. What a put down if I couldn't help myself. Then I realised that though I couldn't put up with pain, death itself didn't disturb me. It wore a friendly face that night and felt like coming home. I can tell this part quite easily. I do not find it so easy to tell what happened next.

I was very content and calm when the doctors came after breakfast. 'Cheer up,' they said, 'you'll be up and out within a week!' Suddenly the telephone rang – it was my mother. 'Lionel dear,' she said, 'the pipes in the loo are leaking, and there's water everywhere. What do we do about it, dear?' My calm collapsed, because household repairs make me panic. I was petulant, self-pitying and tried to pass the buck. When the doctors had gone, I realised I had enough religion for eternal life but not enough for this one: which is a pity for I shall only die once, but the loo will leak many times. It's not the dramatic things of life which test our religion so much as the small daily domestic ones. It was a real professional put down and I brood over it still in my prayers.

# A Muddle of Politicians

My trouble is that as a kid I knew it all. I lived in a part of London that was intensely political, where every weekend, red shirts, blue shirts and brown shirts argued, declaimed, denounced and then threw bricks and bottles. Such certainty was not out of place in the thirties, because a cloud of real evil was spreading out from central Europe.

But after the war there was only a blur. Even left-wingers like me felt the horrors of Stalin, though we didn't yet know the details. Was it right to have dropped the bomb on Hiroshima? If they hadn't, how long would the war in the Far East have continued? I might have been sent there and died in it, which warps my judgment.

As I hitchhiked across Europe after the war, I stopped talking at people, and laboriously started to listen to them. I rolled their words around in my mouth to get their taste as well as their sense, for the finest words can clothe self-interest and anger, and hesitant ones decency.

I don't think religion has the political answers, it hasn't yet done its homework on the insecure, affluent society around it. Every regime in Europe, however nasty, has a religious blessing, which makes ecclesiastical approval somewhat suspect.

So it is only with hesitation I now proffer any help to those who take political responsibility – God help them! I hope some humour eases the burden of the emotions and expectations we put on them. The terrible thing is that on the whole they give us what we want.

# *Our little red flower*

In 1947 I signed on for a student work camp in Yugoslavia because I wanted to experience revolution.

I set off with a war time rucksack festooned with water bottles and useful belts for your bayonets and met other fellow revolutionaries at Victoria, also bearded and bowed under the same war surplus

equipment – we looked like an audition for the hunch-back of Notre Dame.

We sang 'Hail to Tito our Little Red Flower' to urge our train on, for we wanted to reach the future fast. We passed great cathedrals but they were irrelevant. We were more interested in the red flag which we saw run up over a town hall near Turin. Togliatti, the communist leader, had been shot, Italy was in uproar and in Venice all transport stopped. We were stuck. When gunfire not gondolas greeted us on the canals, I dived into a convent where, fretting with impatience, I was given floorspace with some human flotsam left over from the war. There were fascists fleeing to South America, and Ukrainian prisoners of war to whoever would have them. A Dutch deserter was working his way to the Soviet Union, to greet Uncle Jo – God help him!

They pacified me with tomatoes and powdery bread, which was all they had, and I marvelled at their kindness, especially that of former foes.

Well, after some days, a shabby train without toilets did leave the deserted station for the Yugoslav frontier post where the loos were more bourgeois than I bargained for. There were two doors with strange Serbo-Croat inscriptions. In agony, the men hurtled through one and the girls through another and they met head on before a single unisex cabin. Why two doors? Well the Yugoslavs were keeping up appearances – progress demanded it – it was culture. I was touched by their pride and touched even more by the goodness of poor workers or peasants who shared their lunch with me.

For my own pride I could do no less, so when I eventually got back to Venice, I returned to the convent, and I gave away my Yugoslav cigarettes and Slivowitz, my precious mementoes.

Back in London people invited me to parties and asked me 'What is Tito like?' 'He's a little red flower', I said. 'And Yugoslavia?' 'They're poor, proud and kind.' But this was simplistic – I had obviously learnt little abroad and the invitations to parties ceased.

It was true. I still didn't know whether the revolution worked. The Yugoslavs were just too poor to tell, but another kind of revolution had taken place in me, because I was nicer now than when I set out. I think the kindness was catching. The future remained a riddle, but I had touched eternity somewhere en route, in Venice perhaps. It was a fair swap.

So this is my advice: don't dismiss the holdups and delays and changes of plan when you travel this

201 DELAYED

...But I do concern myself about the eternal journey. the air traffic controllers are out.'

summer. Like mine, they may not be accidental for God's hidden hand is at work in them.

# A peep behind the Curtain

The curtain of secrecy and suspicion which separated Europe when I was a youngster is beginning to be dismantled.

I wonder what Europe will be like without it. Perhaps the tourist trade will take a new direction, and instead of Benidorm we will head for Gdansk or a luxury weekend at the Leipzig Beach Hotel.

East Europe will have to readjust too, for when our society was permissive theirs was repressive and they don't produce the goods in the quantity or kind we are used to.

But people don't live by bread alone nor by BMWs, and the proof of it is East Berlin. Now some say it's a grey city, but I've found it rather restful because though they don't produce the goods, they do produce pleasant people who are very polite.

When I couldn't find my coins for the tram, the other passengers pressed their money on me. When I couldn't find the way, people went out of their way to help me find mine. Such things are rare in London, and improbable in Paris.

You also get quality religion in East Berlin. The small Jewish community which meets in a side room of the restored synagogue gives Jews and Gentiles a warm welcome and we all get a hug and kiss from the chairman on Friday evening.

And the cathedrals aren't stiff or snobby. In the east religion brings you no rewards, so people pray in them because they want to pray, and their prayers are pure.

And though you may not find a souvenir, you can bring back a joke instead, because there's a lot of unofficial laughter there – this is one of the latest about the problems of Perestroika.

A Soviet party official is told by Gorbachev in Moscow, 'It's all Perestroika and Glasnost now comrade, and you've got to get used to it. Surround yourself with young bright people. Look, I'll show you,' and Gorbachev called out 'Come over here Sheverdnadze. Show how bright you are. Let's test you! Who's your mother's son who's not your brother?' 'Me,' said Sheverdnadze, brightly. 'You see,' said Gorbachev to the party official, 'now put the new policy into practice.' After the conference, the party official gloomily summoned his deputy. 'Gorbachev says I have to surround myself with young, bright people. How bright are you, I wonder? I'll test you. Who is your mother's son who's not your brother?' 'I don't know. Who is it?' stammered the deputy. 'Well, Sheverdnadze says it's him, but what his reasons are, he didn't say,' said the perplexed party official.

I'll end with an incident which took place at an international youth conference. The delegates from west and east sang 'We shall overcome' and pledged themselves to clean up the world. Only the eastern ones stayed behind to help me clean up the room.

Now, never take God's unqualified approval of your own side for granted, even though you think it's right. Who will God work through in the muddle of the Middle East? Where is This suffering servant? In the Bible His judgments often bewildered His own believers because they contained so much surprise.

# *The over-Promised Land*

I prefer to write about the theology of eternal life, than the politics of this one. But every rabbi has to make a statement about Palestine, Israel, the Holy Land or what you will – so here's mine. I've avoided it so far because the Holy Land is indeed a hot potato which burns the fingers of private people like me as well as politicians, and whatever you write is wrong.

Having said that – the facts are these. It's a small place – the size of Wales – but it's the centre of three world religions and two nationalities, both of which have claims to the whole country and the same capital. Neither nationally could talk to the other because they didn't recognise each other. Jews denied that Palestinians were a people and Palestinians said, 'Israelis are really only a religion' – neither is true. It's a pity only riots not generosity could break the mould of national prejudice.

You can play all sorts of political games with this mess. If I was Arafat and you were Shamir and pussy was President Bush, what would we do?

You can try it out as you read the papers and munch your muesli at breakfast. Your solution won't be worse than the others – federal states, binational states, socialist Soviets and little Switzerland on Sea. All that any of them need to make them work is a bit of trust – but there isn't any.

Both sides are too frightened to be generous and too insecure to give anything up. But until they give something up, neither can get anything.

My own contribution has been modest. With some other clerics we set up the Standing Conference of Jews, Christians and Muslims in Europe. It is a flimsy organisation which staggers from meeting to meeting because it takes no funds from Zionist or Arab sources. Honesty compels me to admit they haven't offered any either. Nevertheless some Palestinian students have met some Jewish rabbinical ones and they've progressed from talking at each other to talking to each other. So I know it's difficult but possible.

Even this most modest contribution arouses huge hostilities. A rabbi hissed 'Arab lover' at me at a meeting in America, but I had the sense to tell this to a Turk who wanted to throttle me, so I'm still here.

Israeli and Palestinian politicians might learn to talk to each other too if they had a little help from religion. But the religions, though creative and courageous, have here behaved like football supporters clubs, each cheering on its own side. They've not helped Jews to recognise themselves in Palestinian refugees and Palestinians to see Jews as another refugee people like themselves. So there's been a religious failure and

Palestine is still called the Promised Land because it was promised to everybody and nobody got it – just trouble.

But things don't have to remain that way. Religion can build bridges between peoples as well as walls that divide them. After all saying sorry and making up quarrels are ordinary domestic miracles you and I manage every day of our lives without much fuss. What makes such lowly problems so hard for the 'higher' religions and nations?

## *Faith in fashion*

A Jewish tourist from Golders Green took a package holiday to China. To his surprise, the guide led him to a synagogue, and he watched the congregation astonished, all Chinese with straight hair and sallow skins. 'Are you really Jews?' he asked the beadle. 'We're very strict Jews,' answered the beadle. 'But please are you Jewish too?' 'Of course,' said the tourist. 'Why do you ask?' 'Well you don't look Jewish,' said the beadle, shaking his head.

Many non-Jews think all Jews look alike. But they don't. They differ in looks and life style.

A semitic face is supposed to be long with high cheek bones. My face is round with low ones, which is normal among the Jews of Russia from whom I'm descended. My mother's parents were very Slav, warm, inconsistent with no sense of time. They ate when they felt like it and I went to bed only when I was tired.

Above us socially lived the Anglo-Saxon Jews who arrived with Hengist and Horsa and dwelt on Hampstead Heights. The men wore brogues and their women twin-sets. We admired their elegance from below and wondered if we would ever be so English.

When I started to study for the Rabbinate, I was taught by yet another group of Jews, different from both, who were appointed to be my teachers. They were the exiled rabbis of Germany, elderly dignified men, who sat around a table, bolt upright on hard chairs, perusing great folios. They failed to teach me what a rabbi should know, because I was too undisciplined and slow. But they did show me what a rabbi should be.

Some had been grilled by the gestapo and never weakened. Some like Rabbi Baeck had gone back to Germany in August 1939 to accompany their communities when they were transported to hell. Some great scholars survived by teaching ignorant schoolboys to read.

Now the war was over, one of them was returning to Germany to lecture. 'How can you,' I asked astonished, 'after what's happened?' 'Mr Blue,' he said, 'when I was a student like you before the first world war, I believed in people's goodness, because everybody did so then and it was easy. But to believe in the goodness of the human heart in Nazi times was very hard, but I struggled, for faith must never depend on fashion.' On Crystal night November 9th, 1938, my teacher's synagogue was burnt to the ground like the others. The broken glass looked like crystal on the street. He was taken off to prison, and his family jeered at by Nazi yobbos. When I visit Berlin I shall remember him and pray. Please God may I be like the good rabbis of Germany. May my respect for fellow men never waver – just like theirs, and my faith never depend on fashion.

## *Pity for politicians*

My mother enjoys people. She talks to strangers, listening to their life stories, because she's really interested. I've caught it from her, because I also sit in stations and hotels watching people – wondering why that stockbroker type is wearing odd socks or that old woman is reading Milton's poems upside down.

That's the reason why I arrive early at the Beeb on Monday mornings. I sit back in the *Today* waiting room fascinated by the famous, dashing through to be interviewed. I've bumped into a lot of them in waiting rooms and wash rooms, and I like the politicians best. They're very polite and as I look like a bag of rags and not a man of the cloth, their politeness must be real. They're more vulnerable than I expected because they like to be liked, which is reassuring. Some are also very tense and some over the top, and I want to hug them, because I'm sorry for them, but don't dare.

I know how hard it is to run a congregation, let alone a country. People tell you to lay down the law, if it's a law they like. They want change with security, and peace with justice, provided someone else picks up the bill. And the politicians must entertain us while they put this muddle into practice. They mustn't converse with each other, but cheer and jeer because a fight's more fun to watch.

A little appreciation from us might work wonders because nobody can do their best without it.

It's wrong to blame others for our own mistakes and talk about 'them' – 'them' being a creed, a class, or politicians. Religion means accepting some responsibility for what happens. I'm saying this because it might help the Soviet and American negotiators if we said thank you for a change, and not use them as convenient dumps for our own anger.

I'm going to give them as my contribution a joke that started off in France. It's politician-friendly because you can adapt it to any party.

The leaders of France, whoever they are, feed their policies and facts into their new supère, dupère, computère. 'What's the French inflation figure in 1992?' they ask eagerly. '1%,' says the computer and they sigh with relief. 'And the unemployment total?' '100,000,' predicts the computer. They can scarcely believe their luck. 'And the price of a French loaf?' one of them asks on impulse. 'Two and a half roubles,' replies the computer!

Now Mikhail can tell it to George, just changing the country, and Barbara can tell it to Raissa, changing the currency. Why Neil could even adapt it for Mrs T and Mrs T for Tony B. It's my contribution to world peace, and I hope radio Moscow and radio Free Europe are monitoring it.

# To the Broadcasting Studio

My broadcasting career began with a disaster. I was so tired after a long journey, I said the first thing that came into my head, which was quite unsuitable. But it was genuine, even if involuntary, and so I was asked again.

I live in a London suburb so my journey to the studio is now much shorter, but a big movement still has to take place inside me before I am ready to talk to anybody, myself and God included.

I start off thinking about what I would be good at saying, what subject I could be witty about. But then I think of the listeners bolting breakfast, and a wave of affection and compassion breaks over me. I begin to worry less about my wit and wisdom and whether I have enough, and more about their needs – not about how to woo them, but how to help them.

Whether the result does help them God knows – and you are a better judge than me. But my 'I' has moved for a few minutes away from my own vanity, and this is the greatest journey I ever experience. Broadcasting has helped me to convert me. I am grateful, and only wish I could keep it up.

# Exodus chapter 4 verse 24

Some of you write to me, 'Rabbi, couldn't I write a *Thought for the Day*?' Sure, why not! Your life's a scripture too, (it's up to you if you want to publish it).

I can certainly pass on some tips about telling it. People are fragile at ten to eight in the morning. So don't make them miserable – it isn't fair. And don't make them laugh while they're shaving – it isn't safe. You've also got to unlearn some Sunday school lessons. The greatest sin isn't adultery, it's taking ten seconds away from a government minister. Now you might think God takes precedence over government. Well He doesn't, and now you know.

But there's a special pitfall in giving a radio sermon, which I didn't suspect at first. You've got one listener more than you bargained for. God is tuning in as well, and taking in every word, and there's a sly smile on His divine countenance.

Now I'm not going nuts. There's a strange text in the Bible which says 'And the Lord laid in wait for Moses and sought to slay him'. Exodus chapter 4 verse 24. Well He's never tried to slay me I admit – I'm not that important, but He's certainly lain in wait for me, just by the door of Broadcasting House in fact.

One morning I was giving a down to earth talk on charity. When I suddenly went over the top and quoted my granny, who said when we meet beggars, we meet God, so we mustn't just give them what we have but also what we are.

Granny's sentiment goes down well and as I prance away, looking for breakfast, I pass the most garrulous beggar in the business. He takes my ten pence and I remember, reluctantly, I have to give him a bit of me too. Could I get him a sandwich? I could – a ham one. At the sandwich bar, the Jewish owner recognises me. I say hurriedly it's for someone else. He looks cynical – so do the customers and I shut up.

The beggar is pleased by his portion of pig and favours me with the story of his life. I can't say 'shut up you silly old b, or I'll bore you out of your silly old mind with mine.' I'm hungry too, and try not to hope he chokes on his ham.

But suddenly a suspicion more horrible than ham crosses my mind. Who is he? When you meet a beggar you meet God! I've just said so to millions, so I have to believe it. The beggar might not realise Whom he's standing in for, but I do. He suddenly wonders out loud where he's going to kip tonight. He knows a sucker when he sees one! I'm hoist with my own petard – it's going to be a long day.

It's dangerous giving a *Thought for the Day* or any religious talk. It's like playing poker with the Almighty, and rashly, raising the stakes.

Thank your lucky stars, you only have to listen to a *Thought for the Day*. If you gave one, you would have to live it too.

# *Going public*

Public problems always push out private ones in the papers and on the radio. But there are some private problems that affect so many people, they deserve to go public too. An example? What about this!

What do you do when you wake in the night and however you try, you can't sleep?

It's a common problem, and an old one. The rabbis said it went back to Adam. He woke up on the first night and couldn't sleep – terrified of the loneliness. But God placed two flint stones beside him, one called darkness and the other death. Adam became curious and struck them together. From the two lifeless stones came a live spark, which he coaxed into flame. He used his own fears to produce light.

And we can use our sleeplessness in the same way. Here are some tips which work with me when I can't sleep. They were passed on to me by other bothered people, and I pass them on to you.

The first thing to do is release yourself from your own expectation. You don't have to sleep eight hours a night – the number '8' isn't need but habit. So if you can't sleep, don't try.

Next get moving, otherwise your room will feel like

a prison, which it isn't, the walls are just mirrors reflecting back your irritation and anger.

To help you face them, I recommend tea and fruit cake. So be prepared, and have a thermos ready. And never despise small things, there's a lot of healing in them.

Now how do you get rid of your anger? The rabbis said you should research the Talmud to find out if you're entitled to be angry. But at 3 a.m. that's beyond me. A counsellor told me to crash cheap plates. But they aren't cheap anymore, even in charity shops and I don't like destruction.

My tip is simple! If you can't sleep, work! – that's what we're put here for.

What work? Anything that helps the world and you, and don't be snobbish! Crocheting is good for women and men. So is writing overdue postcards, so is painting by numbers. Reserve some practical work for sleepless nights.

And reserve some spiritual work too! Pray for people awake like you, lorry drivers, patients waiting for prescriptions, travellers queueing for taxis, people who are praying for you. By praying for them you'll feel part of them and that will relieve your loneliness.

Is this advice relevant when you're going to work, angry and worn out after an interrupted night? Yes! You've got more resources than you realise inside you, of concentration and kindness. Prayer unlocks them, which is why people practise it.

So cheer up and treat yourself to some chocolate. There's a sexist sequel to the Adam story by the way.

When Eve was created she also couldn't sleep the first night. So how did she pass the time. She counted Adam's ribs!

# *Rabbiburger*

It's not easy being natural on the media. Take TV cooking for example. I'm a plump person who perspires under the strong studio lights. To make me look natural, they pat pancake base on to my face and then dust it with flour – like the way I prepare a schnitzel for shallow frying.

On the set I have to prepare meals in minutes and sometimes in seconds, which makes me nervy. While my fingers are fiddling around in a processor, I have to smile sweetly into the camera, looking carefree, though Rabbi's finger, minced and raw, may be on the menu so to speak.

Of course it helps if you have natural grace, but I haven't. When I went to take my dish from the oven, one of the camera crew complained because the viewers got a screenful of my bottom covered with tautly stretched trousers. It wasn't a pretty sight he said, and reminded him of a nature film he'd seen with a shot of young rhinos drinking at a water hole, taken from the rear.

Unintentionally I had my revenge. I boiled a basin of greens in the studio kitchen and then drained them in the studio sink. But the sink wasn't plumbed in, so as well as draining my greens, I drowned the camera crew as well, and my smile turned into a ghastly grin.

Now there are many techniques for appearing natural in such unnatural situations but I've never been taught them. The only solution I know is supernatural. As I wait for the camera – I make a parcel of my longing for success and my fear of failure and try to give the lot to God. I tell Him 'Do what You like with them, it's up to You, for what I think is failure, You might think is a success.' After all, some poor blighter who can't cook might get more confidence, if he sees I'm not so hot at it either and that might be the point of the programme as far as God is concerned.

Time passes quickly in a TV studio and there usually isn't time for proper prayer so I mutter these words to myself instead, which help me to be natural.

> All that I am
> All that I do
> All that I'll ever have
> I offer now to you.
>
> All that I dream
> All that I pray
> All that I'll ever make
> I give to you today.

I recommend these words to you if you've got an exam or job interview today. They might help you as they've helped me because they're the real thing.

# Home call

I sat in a café not far from the BBC and remembered my dog Re'ach, a big black animal, straightforward and sporty, who would have been happy in a Roedean hockey team. When I let her off the lead in the park, she rose in the air like Pavlova and raced exultant, round and round the green, chasing phantom rabbits, and panicking the lovers who lurked among the buttercups.

Then one smiling day in July, when the sky was blue and families were unpacking their lunch, something happened. I let her off the lead and Re'ach did her usual entrechats. Then she ran a few steps, stood still in muzzy thought, and snorted. A yard of pink tongue hung foolishly from her mouth. She pattered towards me and thrust her muzzle between my hands because she was puzzled and needed comfort. She knew in her blood what I knew in my mind, that she would never run again – she was too old.

The sky remained blue and the picnickers fed and frolicked but we had heard something they had not – the first faint notes from on high calling Re'ach home, wherever that is for big black dogs.

In the meantime we trotted back to our earthly home, and I said it with liver, a language she understood. We lived together contentedly for five years longer, and then she died peacefully in her sleep.

I remembered all this last week when I arrived back from Spain, tired but untroubled after a sleepless night in the departure lounge, for the loss of one night's sleep had never worried me before. But this time it did – my elastic had gone! My tiredness made me tip over teacups and the words I wrote didn't make sense. I thought of Re'ach and knew it was my turn to hear the first faint notes calling me home. I wandered into the chapel of Middlesex hospital, and put my soul into God's hands as she had put her head into mine.

And because I am a comfort eater like her, I sat in a nearby café and ordered not liver, but tuna rolls with raw onion, and custard pies.

Never had the custard seemed so smooth and creamy, nor the tuna so tasty. I found my phonecard and rang a friend – never had we felt so close. Life becomes lovelier when it has a frame. Those first faint notes, which had seemed so sad when I first heard them, begin to seem sweet. You can enjoy life when you don't own it and it doesn't own you.

And I remembered a remark I had made in the crowded departure lounge, which was wiser than I realised. A tourist had asked me for information, for I looked sunburnt and Spanish. 'I'm sorry,' I said smiling, 'I'm only a stranger here too.' If you can apply these words to the world, you'll know how to enjoy it.

# *Short Journey –*
# *Big Distance*

The profoundest journeys involve little distance. An underground ticket takes you to Harley Street. You leaf through upmarket magazines, and are ushered into the specialist's consulting room. You are only there for ten minutes, but when you come out your world has changed. You have not just journeyed into another country but into another dimension of being. You sit in a café, and wonder how you can construct another cosmos, for the old one crumbled in the consulting room.

But when you are reconciled to your state, and accept the different destinies of your body and soul, a hospital has its jolly side. There is care and companionship, and endless cups of weak tea. There are also unexpected trips which have their thrill.

I like trolley rides through corridors. I am wrapped in a sheet, and the other patients eye me interestedly. I am interested in them too. There is the same satisfaction as an Italian passeggio or a stroll along the Promenade des Anglais at Nice.

Also when you journey from bed to bed, you eat what the previous occupant ordered the day before. The menu has the same excitement and mystery as the ingredients of a paella on a Spanish Costa.

# I like it here!

I start to feel feeble, and drop in on my doctor who dispatches me to the hospital. They tell me my heart is in the right place, but there's a shadow on my lungs which shouldn't be there.

It might be pneumonia but it might only be my nipples. I strip and a polite nurse puts paper clips on my protuberances. Draped in a toga and two paper clips, I am trundled to 'X-Ray' on a trolley, looking like a Fellini extra or a leftover from Gibbon's *Decline and Fall*. Other patients peer at me which makes me bashful, but they burst into laughter and I resign myself gratefully to the NHS.

I enjoy being institutionalised and wonder if that's why I like package holidays, and rigorous retreats. Perhaps I would feel at home in a prison or asylum, but shan't put it to the test.

I'm grateful for the hospital food which I don't have to prepare or wash up. But I do wonder at the taste of my bed's previous occupant whose menu I now munch. I choose cheery, childhood foods and ask for second helpings of pudding and blancmange which wobble like me.

For a few days I am attached to a drip. I am apprehensive but buck up when a nice nurse compliments me on my juicy veins. A Jew with juicy veins! I get fond of my drip. We go walkabout together, and it's like having my dog back on a lead. I call it Fido. Being clumsy I bang it, and watch my blood flow out of me like raspberry juice. Then I learn to twiddle another knob, and watch with satisfaction my life blood flow back into me again.

I lie awake that first night wondering what's wrong with me. I consider consumption, cancer, Aids and clots. Perhaps I have them all, and I prepare to pass away. As a Minister of Religion, I've comforted dying people, and wonder if I can do the same thing for myself.

Dozing in the darkness, I remember an episode in Italy long ago. I suddenly knew I was no longer loved, and sat in an empty tourist church with an empty

Walkies!

heart. Then something spoke in me and It said, 'In this life you will only see the broken reflections of love in the faces of those who are fond of you. But one day when the world which separates us drops away, you will look into the face of love itself. You will no longer need your mind or imagination to know Me.'

I recall those words, and find to my relief that death does not depress me though pain does. When I gaze into it, it wears a friendly face.

In the morning the doctors tell me cheerfully they'll have me out in a week. I register joy, but really I wish it were a month!

## *Straight question – straight answer*

The letter was short and to the point, which I appreciated. It said:

'Dear Rabbi,
Why do you believe? I would like to but can't.
I enclose a stamped addressed envelope, for your reply.
Yours sincerely.'

My answer was direct but not so short.

'Dear Mrs X,

I don't believe that much or that easily. Our universe doesn't strike me as a kind or cosy place. It used to seem hostile – now it seems indifferent. Probably, I admit, because I think of myself as its centre.

My belief gets some support from scriptures but not as much as I want, because they strike me as a mix of what actually happened, what people wanted to happen, and what people thought was the meaning of what happened. I still can't unscramble them.

But you're right, I do believe, though for practical and very personal reasons. Here's one!

My parents originally wanted me to be a solicitor or a doctor, certainly not a rabbi and I wanted to be a vet. I tried to be a solicitor and it didn't work. Personal problems made doctor and vet both impossible. The first and most important problem was that I couldn't stand the sight of blood. When I went to donate some I passed out, and they told me not to come again – my blood wasn't worth their trouble.

To cure my phobia, I took a holiday job as a ward orderly, and was put on bedpans, but even in the sluice I wasn't safe. I didn't dilute the disinfectant, so my hands came out of the sink without their skins. For one night I ceased to be an orderly living out, but a patient living in.

I also developed another sort of phobia as well, I used to think I'd caught every disease going because my anxiety states were beginning. And that is how I turned up when I was only a school-boy at a clinic for diseases, that middle class people don't mention. The assistants gave me tests and were impressed, though perplexed by my precocity, and I was finally seen by the doctor, who asked me what happened in a business-like tone.

"I kissed a girl," I confided.

"Well what then?"

"I've told you," I explained carefully, "I kissed her."

"But why come here?"

"Because she wasn't a nice girl," I replied worldly wise.

He choked and gave me a cup of coffee and some pamphlets with rather rude drawings, and as I left I heard them all falling about with laughter.

"There's nothing wrong with you," they said – which was only partly true. My body was well enough but my mind was sick with anxiety. As I've said, I learned to live with this illness, but it's never really been cured.

But as a minister of religion I visit hospitals, and hospices and chat to people festooned with tubes, drips, drains and bottles of blood. It's part of my job. How do I forget my own disability and concentrate on theirs? Because when I pray, a power comes to meet me which carries me across the frontiers of my own fear. I believe in it because it works.

I sometimes go along to retreats for alcoholics and drug addicts for company because they plug in to the same power and share the same experience. That's why we all believe.

Yours truly,
Lionel Blue.'

# *The XIth commandment*

In the clinic waiting room we clutch our X-rays and chat about rheumatism, recipes and religion. A politician has recommended the ten commandments over the radio and we in the waiting room approve. 'Great stuff, simple, and basic,' says an elderly man. They're certainly basic, but I'm not sure if they're quite so simple.

There are after all two versions of the ten commandments in the Bible, with different details. And Jews and Christians don't divide them up the same way, so they don't have the same first commandment. Also do adultery and murder have the same meaning now, as they had in the macho society of the ancient world?

One patient facetiously invents an eleventh commandment 'Thou shall not commit thyself' and invites me to follow suit. My eleventh is more serious, though less witty.

I propose 'Thou shalt understand thyself' because if thou dost not, thou canst do so much damage without realising it.

As I sip my Ovaltine that night, I remember one awful example after another.

I remember a religious conference which had ended on a high mystical note, and people got carried away. Later on I learnt many people fell in love at that conference and some unhappy relationships resulted. Only long afterwards did I realise what had happened. Spiritual energy had been released, but some couldn't cope or keep it on that level, so divine love was converted into human love and then into sex. I didn't understand the causes at the time, nor did they, which was a pity as self understanding would have spared them so much pain.

A lady writes to me denouncing opinions she rightly detests. As I detest them too, who is she arguing with? If she understood, she could save herself some stamps.

For the last eighteen years, I've dealt with religious divorce and remarriage. Despite the civil settlements, people fight for the possession of a flower pot, or minute amounts of money. They can't understand that these are just symbols of their hurt.

I fall into the same trap myself. I'm left off a committee, feel hurt, protest and am promptly reinstated. But as I loathe committees, why did I protest? Because I hate being left behind that's all! It goes back to my mother being taken away to hospital without me, when I was a baby, and to the evacuation. But my self understanding has come too late, I am again hoist with my own petard, and have to waste my time on points of order, when I long to be out walking among the daffodils.

Self knowledge requires real humility and courage. It's easier to act out our hang-ups than understand them. But unless we understand them, we'll only repeat them over and over again. And that is why so many religious resolutions never work and nothing changes. The world remains the way it is, and we remain the way we are, despite our prayers and penances.

## *Curing and healing*

Like many middle-aged people, I can't resist recounting the story of my operation.

Last April, I noticed a pain in my chest which wouldn't go away. My doctor referred me to a specialist, who referred me to a surgeon who drew me a diagram which looked like spaghetti but wasn't, just clogged and collapsed arteries. I was convinced and told him to carry on cutting.

On the morning of the operation, I dozed, woke up, dozed again and resurfaced, wondering when they would get on with it. But why was I festooned with tubes? They couldn't have operated already! I dozed again. But they had! During my doze, they had sawn through my breastbone, spatchcocked me like a chicken, transferred a vein from my leg to my heart, clipped my breast bone together, and put me back to bed, hung with drips and drains.

It was an astonishing non-event, and I hope one day dying will be the same.

'Anything on the other station?'

A few days later I stumbled round the corridors, with other gents, in jogging suits and droopy drawers, and ladies in lacy lingerie, all members of the same club with the same scar to prove it. Then I lay back in bed, bewildered by the miracle of modern medicine.

I was also bewildered by what a nice person I had become. I oughtn't to say such a thing, but it's true. One nurse said I was a perfect patient, old resentments faded, broken friendships were resumed, and I only quarrelled with one visitor.

The doctors and nurses had cured my body, but what had healed my soul? Their skill and care were one cause. Also a brush with mortality makes me more real. But the prayers and postcards I received were decisive. When you receive concern and affection, you can't help being nice – even to yourself. Niceness grows in you like weeds.

Curing and healing are closely connected. People get ill for many reasons, among them stress and strain, because they think no one cares enough. Then they try to smoke or drink away their emptiness. Cocooned in other people's prayers I knew I'd never feel unwanted again.

When I got home, the strains of ordinary life resumed. Where had I squirrelled my cheque book? Dare I wear my auntie's garters to keep up my surgical stockings? And my new growth of chest hair was prickly, like King Kong's. Would my new niceness be as sturdy as my new arteries?

I don't know the answer to that one – so I hope my well-wishers carry on praying though more moderately than before of course. When I came out of hospital I resolved to pray for someone else each morning – someone waiting for the same operation, or a hostage who feels forgotten. A postcard might help too. When I used to say prayers for others in services I wondered if it was worth while. Having been at the receiving end, I know it is. I don't understand how it works, but please don't stop!

# Chow

It's after midnight – I can't sleep, twiddle my transistor, and tune in to a religious talk, I hear the same advice I've so often given others (you perhaps). Get up, get out, and do good deeds (see page **138**). But as

I'm fastened to a drip and pacemaker I can't do any deeds good or otherwise – I can only be done to.

If you're bedridden too and feeling useless and frustrated – I recommend to you a curious scripture, neither Jewish nor Christian but Chinese, that helped me.

I came by it when I was up at Oxford in the fifties. The Church of England was as bothered by the South India question then as it is by lady bishops and Bible scholars now. I was fascinated by religious rows, and sat absorbed in chilly church halls, sucking sweets. There I met a Chinese student, equally absorbed, whom I called Chow – though whether Chow was his Christian name, surname, or what he ate, I never knew. He was a sweet, silent chap, whose only outburst occurred in a café. An advert said if you wanted to look special you should use a certain cigarette holder. All the students there were looking special, and sucking the same cigarette holders. Chow became hysterical and couldn't stop cackling.

He vanished from Oxford quietly, leaving a translation of that curious Chinese scripture in my pigeon hole with no note. No one even knows its author's name (I don't know Chow's either) – only his nickname 'Old Boy' – Laó Tse in Chinese.

Look at your window says the Old Boy. The important part isn't the frame, but the hole which lets in the light. Gaze into your teacup! The useful part isn't the container but the hollow it contains. It's the things you don't do, the empty times, which give your life value.

Strange advice, which doesn't just apply to invalids. You go to a prestige party. You want to shine and think of a beautiful bitchy remark. God bless you if you don't say it, and let the others think you're dull.

You're racing your trolley round the supermarket trying to find the fast check out. Take the first fate provides, and don't export your tension.

You're stuck in a hospital bed. Before you summon the night nurse, relax into your weakness. See if the harmony of Heaven works through you!

Some people you don't expect, understand this message instinctively. At Sunday School the clever kids were shouting 'Sir, Sir,' and waving their hands to get my attention. One very clever girl didn't because she thought the unclever ones should have a chance. You have to be very big to be a nobody.

Now all my life I've tried to be a somebody. But in the hospital ward I let go. I was a nobody I knew it, at one with the snuffles from the beds nearby, the whispers of the nurses and the moonlight tumbling through the window. A burden had gone just as Old Boy said. I stopped twiddling and fell asleep like a child.